the
WAITING

Travelling God's route to marital bliss -
A true story.

ANDISWA H. OLUDARE

the WAITING

Copyright © 2018 Andiswa H. Oludare

Cover photograph: John Oludare
Cover design: Eunice Hammond & Prince Adeleke George

Prepared for print by
Preflights Books, Pretoria,
a division of BK Publishing (Pty) Ltd
www.preflightbooks.co.za

www.andiswajezile.co.za

ISBN:
ISBN-10: 0620804998
ISBN-13: 978-0620804998

To the one who loved me first and eternally, Jesus Christ.

Contents

Dear Isaac

The ocean has depth and width which my natural mind cannot comprehend. Yet I know for sure that the tides will mount up pushing to the shoreline. I do not know you yet, I know God in whose heart you are and as sure as His Word is I know He will soon cause our paths to meet.

Whilst He delays our meeting, I pray He keeps you footed at the center of His will. I pray you are well kept in His love always.

Till we meet, I wait on God for you.

Yours,
Rebecca

"Blessed is she who has believed that the Lord would fulfill his promises to her!" Luke 1:45 (NIV)

Acknowledgments

First, I thank the Lord of my life, Jesus Christ, for finding me worthy of His love and making my life such a beautiful master piece. I thank Him for His unrelenting love; He never gives up on me and for that I'm forever grateful.

I thank my husband, John, for waiting for me and choosing to live this life with me. Thank you for your passion for a lifestyle of purity. The Lord knew best in preferring you for me. You are the most beautiful part of my every day and a beautiful expression of God's love for me.

I thank my daughters, Hadassah and Amaris, who ignite faith and the warrior in me. When I look at you, knowing the gifts you are, I want to be all that the Lord has planned for me so that I can better teach you to be all that you have been called to be.

To my mother Lindelwa, my brothers Aviwe and Philande, and my only sister Nenekazi, thank you for being part of my beginnings and my every day. You see me as I am and love me the same. My late father, Tembisile, you demonstrated the sacrifice of love for me in an unforgettable manner. You were my first love and my love for books I first shared with you.

I miss you dearly.

To my father and mother in law, thank you for your prayers, love and support. I am inspired greatly by your steadfast love for God.

To Pastor Femi Joseph Ali, thank you for believing in me and for ever being a willing partner with what God does in my life. You are such a blessing. You preach the Word without compromise and inspire me to be bold in doing the same.

To Pastor and Doctor Magubane, thank you for seeing in me what I believe the Lord placed in me. Thank you for giving me the platform to express the passion to the Lord's Glory.

To Doctor Victor Olujobi and family, your love is consistent and strong. You see me as He sees me and avail yourselves totally to be a blessing. You are heaven's gift throughout and I'm forever grateful.

To Doctor Yomi Oyekanmi, you are one of the greatest teachers I know. Thank you for making me a better teacher of God's Word.

To my friends and the many women I have walked with, young and old, thank you for touching my heart in the ways that you did. I have seen God in your lives and have been inspired to reach out for more. In walking with you I found my voice, my gift.

Foreword

Life is a script, written by God, to be acted by men. It unfolds page by page as events that occupy our daily lives, though unknown to us at the time of their happenings that it is a whole story.

This book is the story of the events of a life, divinely scripted and calculatedly orchestrated to become an epistle for others to learn from.

Andiswa in this book has opened up her life to us in a logical and sequential manner; narrating the events of her life. But more than a story, she has shared valuable principles that formed the fabrics of and have sustained her life. The principles shared in this book were divinely taught to Andiswa by God, though they are not private revelation but universal principles of life, which if well taken and followed by any other person on earth, will produce similar results, if not the same.

Andiswa has shown in this book that the results of our life are like products, which in essence requires processes for formation. And that such processes require waiting. No man who is unwilling to wait will eventually emerge the right picture the Maker has intended. The waiting must not be passive but active; where we consciously glean all the lessons they teach us about life.

Thank you Andiswa for allowing us into your privacy so we could learn cheaply from your hard-earned experiences about life.

I am inviting you all into the School of God , through this book, to learn about the art of waiting so you can be better furnished for the journey of life . This book has much to offer all categories of people in life- young, old, poor, rich, literate or illiterate. Welcome to this world of adventure through "The Waiting."

Femi Ali

Introduction

I was thirty-five years old when I finally said "I do". To anyone who has ever waited for any of the Lord's promises to be made reality, that first line alone ignites mixed feelings: feelings of hope that no matter what one may be going through, the Lord does fulfill His promises. On the other hand, terror at the possibility that the promise could take that long to materialise. Thirty-five is a long time to wait for a promise. I wish that I could say the journey was smooth sailing but I would be lying. Maybe if I had been a saint it could have been, but I was pure flesh and blood, imperfect in all ways. I desperately needed God's grace to wait right.

I have experienced the intensity in the journey to marriage. Layers beneath my lovely face and smile are monumental scars serving as testaments to depth of this journey. I am now thirty-seven years old and when I look back at the past years I am overwhelmed by how His love and grace preserved me. I know without a doubt that I would not have been able to hold on to His promise until the end if He had not been such a keeper of my soul.

I had the honour of being taught many things during the waiting season by the Lord. I have seen and experienced how, without the right perspective, this season could lead one away from Christ. I have also seen how the right foundation can make the waiting season a period that develops in a person attributes that carry one throughout life. The experience birthed in me a deep passion for all who are still in the waiting season for marriage and by God's grace He has opened my eyes to some tools for waiting right. I believe that God birthed this in me by making sure that I first walked the journey so that I would carry the scars myself. The Word of God tells us that Jesus is our High Priest. He was tempted in every way, just like us, and because of that He is able to identify with our struggles and also help us into victory.

For we do not have a high priest who is unable to empathize with our weaknesses, but we have one who has been tempted in every way, just as we are – yet he did not sin. Hebrews 4:15 (NIV)

So, sometimes God will allow us to experience certain things in life in order that we may learn and, having learned, comfort others with the same comfort we have received. I believe that when you have crossed to the other side it is your responsibility to pass the boat back for the safe crossing of others.

This book will draw from experiences, my own and of those whose lives I have watched even from afar. There are many ways by which we can learn invaluable lessons in life. We can learn by going through the process, getting burnt along the way, and coming out with scars to testify. Or, we can learn by careful observation of other people's lives. In this book I hope to take you on a journey where you will hopefully learn from the mistakes that many of us have made. Should you find yourself already in any of the situations described here, I pray that the Lord would meet with you in a specific way and set you free. We serve a God whose name is Faithful; He is interested in even what seems to be the smallest detail of our lives. As you read on please open your heart and allow Him to address those deep issues within.

Waiting on the Lord is a process that all of us will go through in our journey with God. We wait for admission to pursue our desired careers, we wait for jobs, for finding the right marriage partner, and to conceive children – just to name a few. I have seen that to God it is not so much about our sense of having arrived, or receiving the promise, rather it is about the development of Christ-like character in us.

You see, the career choice that I laboured to attain for years is a simple thing with God, as was the gift of marriage. In one word the Lord would have blessed me with these desires but what would that have achieved? Happiness of His daughter which, as we know, would not have lasted because soon enough we complain about the very things we cried to God for. Soon enough I would have come to Him asking for more and more. What would I have learned from never having to wait for anything? Not much.

There is a lot of transformation that happens in us when we wait on the Lord. Mindsets that have become strongholds go through a reshaping and it is only at the end of the season that we get to see what the Lord was making in us and marvel at the beauty of our inner man. The waiting season has no respect for anyone – degree holders, young and old, the lofty and the low – all come face to face with it. Once we have yielded to its pruning we get to realise that what we hunger for is not as precious as the priceless value of having God in our lives. We learn to celebrate the Giver first and everything that He gives becomes secondary. We learn to be content and be thankful for the gifts that He has already blessed us with. We learn endurance and the ability to stand and proclaim Christ, even when our bodies want to quit. We learn to choose His will over our own. The attributes developed in these seasons are priceless and only such hearts that have been tested and can be trusted are usable by God.

The beauty of scars from the waiting season became something that distinguished me from many and also molded me for God's plan. This is my story and I hope in the next pages you will not only find a story to relate with but also that you will find hope and strength to soar higher than you have before.

The beginnings

I was twenty-four years old when I decided to give my life to the Lord. I am still not quite sure why I had resolved to remain a virgin until marriage prior to giving my life to Jesus Christ. I think it was a couple of factors that came to play: I had grown up in a catholic boarding school where I first learned about God, heaven, and hell and I really did not want to dishonour God and end up in hell. Also, I remember being accused of being loose and therefore it seemed I was most likely to sleep around and fall pregnant because of my friendships with people of opposite sex. The perception that I was beautiful only fueled these speculations.

I have always had a strong will and this helped me to defy the odds many times. As a young girl in my early teens I vowed to myself that I would not have sex until I became married, amongst other reasons to prove that I was my own person able to pioneer my own path. This did not mean that I would not date; I believed in love and finding the 'one' person who would be my husband. I had read about this kind of love in books and had held my breath watching movies that told stories of happily ever after. I wanted this kind of love and my decision to abstain from sex meant that I could not be in a relationship just for the sake of dating, I wanted to be with someone I saw myself getting married to. I refused to be with someone who could not go the long run with me without indulging in sexual intercourse. I made this clear from the onset and, needless to say, this shortened the lifespan of many of my relationships. As one person expressed, I was "fishing from a very small pond". She may have been right but I was not willing to compromise my standards for anyone, not even for my heart's desires. However, as years passed I became confronted by the reality that this strong will I prided myself in could only take me a certain distance and not the longest mile.

I have blogged about 'life in the shades of grey'. I use this term to bring attention to the realities that life as we know it often does not follow the patterns we draw up innocently when we are young. Take a young teenager and ask them what they envision their life to look like at the age of thirty. On average you will get a picture of having qualified with a high-paying job, owning a car, a house, being married with a child or two, and having travelled the world. This average girl knows that working hard is part of the perks when one desires a good life. To this young girl the world is full of many possibilities and the idea that her dreams may not come true as pictured is far-fetched.

Many of us had dreams painted in our minds and hearts until life happened in its reality. By the age of thirty many of us have volumes of books detailing dreams that never made reality, stories of detours and broken canvases. Some are still trying to put those beautiful pictures back together, others have remained stuck in that place of shattered dreams whilst some have learned to bend and find a masterpiece hidden in the detours of life.

I was this young girl whose dreams came crashing down as soon as I left high school. Life definitely threw a curve ball at me and not only did I struggle to find out who exactly I was, my dreams of becoming a pharmacist crumbled to dust. I was determined and kept moving, trying to find a path that would lead me to my dreams. The more I tried, the more complex things became. I will open up a bit more here so that the picture I am trying to paint can be clearer.

I passed my matric with good grades that qualified me to pursue a university degree. Mathematics and Physical Sciences were not my strong points but I did well enough. I had not applied for admission at any university, it was only when I received my results that I travelled to another province to start applying. My family worked really hard and spent a great deal of money taking me from one university to the next but the Schools of Pharmacy were closed. We eventually found one university that was still open for a Bachelor of Arts degree and I was told that with my first year results I could apply for a Bachelor of Pharmacy degree. I was desperate to start studying because it seemed that this would give me a sense of direction.

We had heard of many cases where young people stayed at home after matric and I had concluded that this was definitely not my portion.

One year later I applied for a Bachelor of Pharmacy degree and I was told that my grades for Mathematics and Physical Science from matric were not good enough. This time I was advised to register for a Bachelor of Science degree as this would be considered for a Bachelor of Pharmacy degree if I do well. Needless to say, that was the worst year of my life with much happening that affected me psychologically. To make matters worse, I received a letter from the School of Pharmacy before I even wrote my final exams that I was not admitted for the following year.

I threw in the towel; nothing seemed to go right. I felt so lost and the canvas I had once painted with beautiful dreams looked marred. The one thing I had feared the most as a young girl was fast becoming my reality. I had no bright future and for what became a month-long moment, I concluded that it was over. I had failed.

I was ashamed because my parents worked hard to get me where I was. Too many sacrifices had been made to afford me education and this opportunity that amounted to nothing. I was ashamed before my peers, those I went to school with who were now going into third year pursuing careers. I contemplated taking my own life but that picture of heaven and hell hit me again. Instead, I ran away from home to a province I had never been to. I changed my contact details so that I could be out of reach. This way I would not have to answer to anyone and relive the shame.

I was found by two women who are to this day very precious to me. I lived in their home and even though it was a shack, it was full of love and acceptance. They looked after me for a long time until one day when I took a look at where I was and had a deep longing within. On examination I became aware of the stark contrast between what I saw with my physical eyes and the beautiful picture inside of me detailing where I could be. A new hope arose within, strength and will surged in my soul.

I made a resolution to stand once again, to fight on until what I saw within me became my physical reality. I decided to upgrade my Mathematics and Physical Science grades. I found an upgrading school that was far from where I was staying. This posed a challenge because I had no money to rent an apartment, having run away from home.. The ladies I lived with paid for my registration at school as a loan and a friend I had met at university put me in touch with her brother who was working for the South African Navy. Her brother, Mpho, was supposed to help me with accommodation for the duration of my studies. However, he informed me that he would not be allowed to live with me but said that he had spoken to a friend of his who would be able to help me. He was married and was an elder at a reputable church.

I was a girl from the rural areas, raised in Catholic boarding schools, during both primary and high school, and my experience with the city was recent. Many had called me naïve and some innocent. To the innocent, all things are innocent. I say this not to justify anything I did but to explain why I easily trusted people before my exposure to the ills of this world.

I was happy to have found people who were willing to host a stranger in their home. When I arrived, Theo, the married man, told me that his wife and children had recently moved to another province and that he was now living with another young man who had come to the city to work. He continued to emphasise that he was a respectable man of God with a position in the church. I was given the keys for the house and I was grateful. However, I felt cautious to be careful how I dressed since I was living with only men.

I resumed classes the following day and for a while everything seemed to be going well. I would wake up early and take a train to and from school because the house was quite far from where I was schooling. It wasn't too long before I started noticing that my towels were moved from the place where I hung them after bathing and this left me unsettled. I then saw that my suitcase had been opened and that someone had gone through my clothes. I started panicking but convinced myself not to make much of it. It was not long after this that Theo came to my bedroom. He had told me that there were no keys to the rooms, including bathrooms, and I was unable to lock my room. He tried to force himself on me and when I tried to fight him he became aggressive. I closed my eyes and spoke to God, reminding Him that as a young girl I made a promise to Him to stay a virgin until marriage and that I needed Him to keep His side of the promise. Too much had been taken away, I needed Him to preserve this one thing for me and He protected me from this man. God heard my cries and protected me from being raped by him.

I had to get out of there, but where could I go? I couldn't tell Mpho; would he even believe me? Part of me blamed myself for this whole thing, but another part felt that he was justified in offering me a place to stay. I was young and naïve to have believed that the world was a safe place. Layer by layer my innocence was peeled by brutal experiences.

Theo did not try to force himself on me again for some time and I convinced myself that it had all been a mistake and I should never mention it but the next time he came to my room was the last straw for me. I had come back from school and the young man we were living with was not around. Theo came to my room again and tried to force himself on me. That night I couldn't sleep, fighting him off. When he finally went to his room it was the early hours of the morning. I knew then that I could never come back to that house. My life was in danger and I refused to stick around to see what he would do next.

I called Mpho and told him the whole story. He was infuriated and in disbelief. We agreed that he would accompany me to the house to fetch my clothes. I went in first so that Theo would not know that I had company. This would prove my allegations as Mpho would be listening outside the door. I confronted Theo about his abusive sexual behaviour and he did not deny it until my Mpho walked in.

I am a person of words and in my life I have seen how words have the potential to destroy who I am and how they also hold the power to build me up. That day as we were packing my clothes Theo accused me of being sent by satan to lure a righteous man. He said I was an agent of satan himself sent to destroy his family. This stuck with me for the longest time and slowly I started to believe that I had no part in the Kingdom of God. If I was who he was saying, then how could God want anything to do with me?

I left Theo's house as a different woman. He had stolen from my innocence both physically and verbally. I could never look at life the same way and to a great extent I could not look at myself the same way after this experience. It seemed to me that life was trying to destroy all sense of worth in me. Had it not been for God's grace I would have believed that Jesus' death on the cross was not enough to save a sinner like me. I would have believed Theo's words as they stripped me of my self-worth and gone straight into the arms of waywardness. Thank God for watching over me and preserving what needed to be kept. Thank God for coming to the rescue and wiping off every negative word spoken or written on the receptacles of my young heart. He came and re-wrote my story with His mercy at the right time.

I had lied to my Mpho and told him that I had arranged to stay with friends from school. I chose a random destination and he offered to drive me there and gave me R10. It was all he had but it wasn't enough for my journey to nowhere. At the station I looked around and found a bench to sit on and put my small suitcase next to me. I felt stuck, not sure what my next move would be. I couldn't go home, I had not spoken to my family in months, and I only had R10 to my name. None of my friends from school were able to accommodate me. The time for the last train was approaching and I sat there, unsure what to do and wondering if God saw me at all.

Two men from the Congo came and sat next to me as I waited for the last train. They were friendly and started a conversation with me. One of them asked me where I was going and without even thinking I replied, "I don't know." At first they thought I was joking but I continued to tell them that I had no place to stay. At this point I figured I did not have many options. I could sit there at the station like the homeless child that I had become and risk far worse being done to me by men who saw me stranded on the streets or I could decide to trust again.

They told me that they were renting a house with their other brother and sister who had just moved to South Africa from the Congo. They had been looking for a woman who can share a room with their sister as she was still a teenager and needed female guidance. They asked if I would be willing and without hesitation I agreed. I decided to take yet another step of faith.

At their house these two explained the situation to the eldest of the three brothers. He looked at me as if to study me and asked me questions. I had developed a habit of lying about the real story that brought me to this province and no one knew about my family. Luckily they did not want too much detail; they were satisfied with the few words I had given and that suited me. The Congolese men told me that they would observe me over a few days and if they saw a behavior of partying and promiscuity they would ask me to leave their home. "Fair enough," I thought to myself as a wave of relief swept over me. I knew that I had found a place for the rest of the year.

One of them, Flora, payed closer attention to me. They did not eat the same food as South Africans and when he noticed that I was starving he would scold me for not communicating and buy me bread and eggs. I lived on bread and eggs for the most part of that year. He helped me with a weekly ticket to school and later advised me to find a part time job and stop wallowing in my sorrows. I found a waitressing job and this helped me a great deal financially.

I was a child of many sorrows and that soon became evident in my countenance. Sometimes I locked myself in the room and cried my heart out. At these times I struggled to find the answers to why I existed on earth. Often I questioned the very decision I had made, wondering what was wrong with me. I would often ask myself how I ended up there. Have you ever sat down to have a real look at your life and shuddered at the obvious? When I did I felt beaten and defeated. I drowned in my own pain and I felt crippled at the thought of sharing my story. The pain was unbearable but sometimes I learned to survive through it. I learned to not nurse the pains that life had brought me but to step on them and continue moving forward.

In the early part of the year I heard that my father was in the same city I was in, that he had come to look for me. I was so touched by the news and had to make contact with him despite my shame. I remember meeting him at the taxi rank. Apparently he had travelled by bus 1,109 kilometers for fifteen hours. When I saw him my heart was broken. He looked as though he had aged so much since I last saw him. I wanted to throw my hands around him and cry bitterly but I held back and I could see he was also holding back the pain. What had I done to my father, to my family! My heart was racing and torn at the same time. He asked me to please go back home. I was tempted to say yes and pack up my small bag.

He had heard many stories about me, none of which were true. Amongst other stories, he had heard that I had run away with a married man. Oh my heart! How I desperately wanted to explain to him that what people were saying was mere gossip.

"It's all lies, tata" was all my lips wanted to scream out. I could not find the strength to. Instead, I chose to live with the shame of being perceived as wayward by the one man I loved the most in the world. I told him that I was not ready to go back home, that I needed to finish what I was trying to achieve there. It was such a painful moment, seeing how much pain I had caused them all. After a few minutes we said our goodbyes.

Was I wrong to have left home? If I had not left what would have changed, would I have survived the shame? If I went home now in the middle of school would that accomplish anything? So many questions came to my mind. I had to live with the decisions that I had made.

I continued to work as a waitress and study. At the end of that year I went back home to face it all. I knew that I had accomplished something for myself and I prepared my heart to face whatever would come my way. I was welcomed home like the prodigal son. I bless the Lord for my parents.

Year four post matric my parents and I decided I could try again, still for a Bachelor of Pharmacy degree. Once again I headed to yet another province having not applied with the same result: applications to study towards a Bachelor of Pharmacy degree were closed. Instead of going home or applying for another course I decided to do a bridging course at university.

I was twenty-three years old at this point, having finished matric four years ago. I had cut contact with my former school mates and for those who could still get hold of me I was a laughing matter. I figured the only way that I could change this was by taking drastic measures. I have never to this day worked as hard as I did that year. I wanted distinctions in all subjects and this required great effort and focus. The university buzz passed me in oblivion; I ate and breathed my books. It paid off as I received my results at the end of that year.

This time around I had done things right and applied on time. I also decided to apply for Medicine just in case. In January of year five post matric I was waiting for a response from the School of Pharmacy. The fear of rejection which had become so attached to my name crept in. My parents also felt it as they, too, had taken a leap of faith with me. Many times when I dared to take a close look at what was really going on knots would begin forming in my belly. What was I really doing? What if things didn't work out again, despite how hard I had worked? What was wrong with me, had I escaped reality and slipped into insanity, bringing my parents along?

I met a friend of mine at church who poured fuel on the existing fire within. She told me to stop wasting my parents' money and putting them through misery as I pursued dreams that were not coming true. This hurt me in ways that I cannot explain. I needed exterior voices to encourage me, to tell me that I was on the right path but nothing came. All I had was this small hope within. It was so small that the idea that I was banking my life on it was ludicrous.

One day a letter arrived in response to my application for Medicine. As my dad and I looked at each other we both knew what was going on inside each of us: a crippling fear made visible by my trembling hands as I attempted to open that envelope. By now I knew which words to look out for and not waste time torturing myself with the greetings on the letter. The application was rejected. When I saw this response, I held back the tears and told my parents.

They both kept quiet and I knew what I carried in my heart then was exactly what they felt deep inside. I could not bear the pain I was causing them anymore and I could feel that even I had reached the end of myself. I could not take the self-torture anymore. Slowly I walked away even though everything in me screamed "Run!" The past few years had trained me to bottle pain within, to never show how I was feeling. I had seen that being vulnerable does not guarantee that you will be met with compassion. Other people will capitalise on it, they prey on victims.

I remember going to my parents' bedroom and slowly closing the door behind me. I could not stand as I had hoped to, slowly with my back against the wall I slid to the floor. At first a weird sound let out, a groan I had never heard before. I hardly recognised it was coming out of me until tears ran like a river. All the tears I had bottled up inside for the past four years caught up with me. I crumbled with what seemed like an emptying from the core of my belly. My body shook uncontrollably as I drowned in my own misfortune in life. Moments later my mother walked in. She is a tough one, yet, on that day, I saw something I had questioned before: how much love she had for me. She didn't shed one tear but the look in her eyes, the tone of her voice, spelled out the agony of a parent who has watched their child go through a rough road.

"Whose child would you rather this happened to? *Tshotsho yenzeke kuwe Andiswa mntwana wam.* Now you are going back to the same university and when you get there you will apply for whatever they can take you for. You will study hard and excel. Whatever you choose to study know this: your father and I are behind you a 100%."

These words became a bridge of hope for yet a brighter future, my soul found healing and restoration. I found forgiveness and acceptance. Nothing could ever fully express what it means to have the full support and love of those you love. To find love genuine enough to pick you up and dust you off, finding worth in you that your own eyes fail to see. This gives one such an incredible charge and strength to run once again, to try once more.

The following day I packed my bags and my new-found strength and headed back to the university. I had only left home for less than two hours that day when I received the phone call that broke the ground of my misfortune. It was the School of Pharmacy and Pharmacology from the same university that I was heading to. They told me that I had been accepted into my first year. This is one of the moments I would never forget in my life. I was in awe, shaken to tears, oblivious to the taxi I was in and the other passengers in it.

All went silent as I tried to wrap my mind around this news. I had lost so much to get here. I was once a bold, confident girl whose pride and sense of being was defined mostly by beauty and all the fame it brought me. I was that girl who was not afraid of studying hard to get a good degree. These were some of my main strengths and the past four years had destroyed all sense of self-worth. I had gained weight over the years and the most dreaded pimples and acne developed on my face. I felt ugly and dreaded being looked at by anyone. I was ashamed of who I was. I had been stripped of pride and left feeling naked.

I remember walking to the library one day and as I approached four boys were standing at the entrance. One must have said something that caused all of them to turn and look at me. I hated that moment with everything in me. I started sweating everywhere and my body started itching in those few seconds that seemed like an eternity. I did not want to make it obvious that I was nervous so I propelled forward, dreading that I had to make a way between them to enter the library. Just then, my insensitive phone rang and at first I ignored it but it seemed to be drawing more attention to me. In nervousness and embarrassment, I took it out of my pocket to answer it. "Hello," I said, only to have the boys break out into laughter at me. Only then I realised that I had been so nervous and ashamed that they were staring at me that I forgot to press answer on the phone. I had answered the phone whilst it was still ringing! That is how low my self-esteem had been.

Receiving that acceptance letter was a step towards restoration. I held back tears of joy. I had been rejected many times and each time it left a dent in me. Each time it seemed to take away a piece of me. I had endured failure, pain, and shame until I recognised them as a cloth tailor-made for me. The pursuit of a career made hardships part of my identity. Other people are blessed and goodness just falls into their laps but this was not me. I was cursed to toil and bruise before I would have good coming my way, or so I believed.

My acceptance was a game changer for me and my family. I was the first in our family to go to a tertiary institution both in my mother's and father's house. I was seeking to be the first to obtain a degree at university level. God was going to break this generational curse through me and it obviously came with a lot of fighting. That acceptance letter was a crown of victory in every sense and deep down I knew that there was more to come. I was both excited about the dream coming true and at the same time terrified of the unknown.

The lost, found, and redefined

Growing up in the rural areas allows one to learn certain things that one can later infer personal principles for life on. We planted maize and beans at home in our huge garden and in the fields. During the planting season one of the important steps taken before laying the seed on the ground is cultivation of the soil. This is the process of breaking up the soil in preparation for sowing or planting. This was necessary because the ground or soil would have been left for a long time without sowing anything on it. In some cases, it would be soil on which nothing had ever been planted on before. This means that the ground would be really hard, uneven, and even contain stones. This ground would need digging and turning of the soil. Once this is done the soil would be regarded as fertile to plant seeds on.

The hardships that I had gone through in life had wrecked me to say the least, destabilising any sense of identity I may have been clinging to while growing up. A huge part of me had drawn identity from my physical looks and the attention that this evoked. I had grown up in a family where love was not expressed the way we see it on television, being told you are loved and pampered with words of affirmation and physical touch. As a child one tends to yearn for these things, believing that those were the only means of expressing love. Just because my parents did not express their love this way I concluded that I was not loved and the danger of being a young girl growing up with an empty love tank is that one tends to look for things to fill the tank somewhere else.

We are prone to building up this ideal in our minds that we will only be complete once we find love. Our myopic view of love limits us from seeing the sacrifice that parents make to put food on the table, a roof over our heads, and sending us to schools better than the ones they attended. They may never say the words "I love you" but their love resounds in the scars they bear, their selfless way of carrying our deepest pain as their own and how they choose us over themselves often, if not always. The way our parents show love is not always expressed in the ways we understand, and sadly it takes many of us years to realise just how radically we have been loved all along.

Over the years I have learned to respect my parents and esteem highly their love for us. I have cherished the memory of my father coming to my bedroom in the early morning whilst I was still sleeping. I used to hate feeling he was disturbing my sleep by wanting to have small chats. Now I see it as a great expression of love for a man who was never raised to tell his daughter "I love you". I have learned to adore the wrinkles on my mother's face for they tell me a story of continually sacrificing yourself for the benefit of those you love.

My parents sacrificed a luxurious life growing up, they sacrificed scrumptious meals and fancy clothes because they chose to give us a better education. My father was a salesman for an insurance company and that meant that he needed to own a car to meet potential clients. When I was finally accepted for a Bachelor of Pharmacy degree he sold his only car to pay for my registration and school fees. He had to take taxis and walk for a year, if not more. What a sacrificial love! This is better than a thousand professions of love without the sacrifice. I did not know all this then and such lack of knowledge misled me to a path that almost destroyed me. I felt empty of love and it was my mission to find the kind of love I believed I never had.

I had also rested on dreams for career qualification to give me purpose. I thought that having a career was the key to a good life, that it would give me a sense of importance in the community. All these dreams came crashing down one after another within the space of four years. All that once stood as my pillars was uprooted and it was a devastating thing to not just witness but to experience this. I was that hard soil for so long, full of pride. By the end of the four years I was left feeling lost, fearful, and vulnerable to say the least. These experiences had cultivated my life, removing the hard part of my heart and exposing the soft part, preparing it for planting and growth in dimensions unfamiliar to me. God loved me enough not to leave me to my own destructive ways. I could never fully explain the profound effect of being loved this way. God allowed pain and loss to bring out fertile ground ready for His seed.

As I celebrated finally being a first year student pursuing my dream career, I soon realised that it was a journey on its own that I couldn't just glide through. I was in the making and the process was far from over. I had to plug into the journey and bend with each curve of challenges. I was determined to make it. I was immediately confronted by the reality that I would be the oldest in the class but thank the Lord who answers prayers. He had preserved my youth for me so much that most people could not believe it when I told them my age. Still, the knowledge of this affected me and I had to learn to embrace it. It meant that I would never get prospects for marriage in my class and, sadly, at my church as well. I also had to embrace that my highschool mates were ahead of me in life, in an entirely different league.

If people decided to laugh at my case, I learned to find humor in what they were laughing at and at the names I was called in the process. I learned to keep my story before me so that I didn't sway and forget that I'm not like the rest. I kept very few friends and focused on my books.

As days progressed I couldn't act oblivious of the void within that seemed to grow daily, this emptiness within that I couldn't fill with anything even though I tried to. I tried to distract myself by watching television, reading a book, catching up with a close friend, or even calling home. These things would bring happiness but soon it would go away and that deep longing would return again.

Society teaches us many things and expects much from us. I had lived my life trying to reach societal milestones for normal growth and evidently had fallen far behind. I had to learn to find my truth and live by that truth and yet it seemed blurry. Obtaining a qualification and finding the right man to settle with in life, getting married, and having children suddenly left a feeling of unfulfillment within. Deep down there was an undefined pain that became pronounced with each passing day. Soon I realised that it was a deep yearning for more – there had to be more and my soul panted for it.

Tertiary life is ground full of adventure, thrill, and excitement as it offers freedom for all. Many people let loose because for the first time they are on their own, away from supervision of any kind. Identities are formed while some are broken as one's eyes are opened to many possibilities. One's stand and beliefs will be tried and tested. Everything that was once considered forbidden is suddenly permissible and enjoyed by many. Alcohol and drug consumption, parties, co-habiting, and same sex encounters, to name just a few, become the culture of the new environment.

As strong-willed as I had considered myself to be, I soon found my own strength failing. My stand on abstinence until marriage was tested most of all. It was not something to be celebrated but rather I faced ridicule often times. I had to make people understand why I was still a virgin at my age. What had once been a bold declaration soon became a faint response accompanied by a grin of confusion. I was getting used to being mocked for the decisions I had made in my life. My confidence was thinning as I found myself asking the same questions internally. Eventually I could not think of one reason why I should not just give it up and blend in, it seemed that everyone else was doing it.

One day while walking from the lecture rooms to my residence, I was deep in thought about this particular subject. A young man came from behind me and started chatting me up. Within minutes he addressed the issue of young girls who come to university sexually pure and eventually succumb to peer pressure. I was amazed as he continued convicting me about losing one's moral behavior. The conversation with this man touched me. When I got home I called my friend's mother and told her about my contemplation since I had no strong reasons for abstaining.

Do not give dogs what is sacred; do not throw your pearls to pigs. If you do, they may trample them under their feet, and turn and tear you to pieces. Mathew 7:6 (NIV)

This is the scripture verse which my friend's mother quoted. It reignited something inside of me. Sexual intercourse is sacred and the act was designed by God to be performed within the marriage context. Any sexual activity between two people who are not a married man and wife defiles the body. There are three institutions that were created by God: marriage, church, and government. The coming together of a man and woman sexually was created by God, He is the wisdom behind it. Satan perverts everything that God creates and because of this anyone who subscribes to Satan's perverse ways is prone to suffer the consequences of such a choice. It takes the grace of God to protect us from many things that could have been the consequences of our misuse of God's divine gifts.

Dogs and pigs cannot understand what is holy, what is sacred. Their nature is not designed to comprehend it and because of this we are not supposed to give to them what is sacred, expecting them to treasure it. When you give your body, which is the temple of God, to a man or woman outside the context of marriage, you are opening yourself up for violation. Society has misinformed many into thinking that having sex with someone causes them to love you more. If this were true, then everyone would be with the person that they first gave themselves to. They would not sleep with you, say they love you, and then go to someone else afterwards. My decision was made and it did not matter what anyone said after this.

However, the need to know who I was and why I was born grew more and more. The questions lingered without any answers. I used to attend church, although not regularly, but every time I went there was a comforting sense of hope and joy that would come over me. I later noticed that I had the same feeling when I was in my own room playing worship songs. I would pray to God and worship Him. The idea of being a born again Christian was not really appealing to me for a long time. Amongst other things it seemed to me to be for people who did not want boyfriends, people who always covered their hair and wore long dresses, even in winter.. Those were unhappy people and I definitely did not belong to this click. However, after I was admitted to study towards a Bachelor of Pharmacy degree I knew that God had heard my prayers. My heart was warming up to God.

It was one Sunday morning while I was in my room that I felt God's presence as I listened to worship music. He had come to meet me. I remember breaking down and crying a river, being overwhelmed by the sense of being loved by Him. My whole life played out in my mind as if it were a movie as I lay flat on the floor. I saw Him being there when I was born, I saw His love raising me as a child, it was His face shinning on me each time strangers found favor in me. He had been there protecting me the nights of attempted rape when I was vulnerable. He chose to honor a little girl's request for Him to preserve her virginity. He had been the stranger who made sure I never went to bed hungry and He had made sure that I always had a roof over my head. He had been the assuring voice in the midst of the storms. He had been my victory until this moment.

I had looked for love everywhere, almost jeopardising my life in the arms of boyfriends. I had searched for acceptance and belonging and came to nothing.

At this moment as I dared to look at Him, I saw the Man who had always loved me, who had pursued me when I could not even give Him a second thought. Love found me that morning and redefined me. Overcome by the strength of His love I gave myself away without holding back; I was captivated by the love of the one who knew me before I was even born. I uttered a prayer of surrender, acknowledging that He is Jesus Christ and Lord who came from Heaven to die for sinners like me. With my heart, my voice, and my soul I chose Him as my Lord and savior. I surrendered all to Him.

As I lay there on the floor with my face in the pool of tears I couldn't have missed the newness I sensed deep within. It was as if everything went quiet, within and without. I was lighter and feeling like a child without a care in the world. I was made alive, resuscitated from death to life. I realised then that I had been blind and at that moment scales fell from my heart and I began to perceive myself even as I am known by Him. There is no greater love that the one God gives, this my soul knows too well. It was in Him I would find my identity and purpose for being born. He was the fountain of living waters that my soul was longing for and He filled my heart to the brim. I felt loved, beautiful, and complete!

The Father's child

The Lord led me to a church where I would fellowship until I left university after having qualified in Pharmacy. The pastor did an alter call for anyone who wanted to give their lives to the Lord and also for Baptism in the Holy Spirit. I knew that the Lord wanted me to go and seal before congregational witnesses what He had done in the privacy of my room. So, I walked to the front and that Sunday in March of 2005 I was baptized in the Holy Spirit and spoke in tongues for the first time.

In January of the year preceding my salvation I had finally agreed to date a young man that I had known since I was in first grade. I had known him for years and I felt that it was okay to date him at that time since he was based in another province far away from me. This meant that there won't be any distractions to my studies. After accepting Jesus to be Lord in my life I still continued with the relationship. I would go to church, read my Bible, and spend time alone with God.

We met a few times that year and things got physical, we were kissing and fondling, but we had both agreed to no sex before marriage. Still, I couldn't shake the ugly feeling I would get afterwards and I did not fully understand what it meant. I started thinking that maybe I was not attracted to men. I continued going to church and professing salvation. I was convinced that there was nothing wrong with being physical that way. We had limits and I was still a virgin, therefore I would talk guilt out of my mind. Surely the Lord had to be proud of me, right?

It was only late that first year that I felt a deep desire for more of God in my life. I wanted more of Him, I wanted to give Him all of me. I started sensing that the Lord did not want me to date until the time that He would lead me to the man who would be my husband. I finally learned that the ugly feeling was in fact what we get when we are indulging in sin and grieving the Holy Spirit.

May God himself, the God of peace, sanctify you through and through. May your whole spirit, soul, and body be kept blameless at the coming of our Lord Jesus Christ. 1 Thessalonians 5:23 (NIV)

Mankind is made up of body, spirit, and soul (mind, intellect, and emotions). We are spirits in a body with a soul. When we are saved, our spirits are born again, meaning that our spirit man becomes 100% new and holy after the image of God. It is in our spirits that God dwells and communicates with us. The moment I was saved my spirit hated all forms of evil, or sin, and that is why I struggled with certain behaviors that had become habits before salvation. We all know that old habits die hard and I had to go through the process to unlearn old ways and imbibe the new ways that are led by the Spirit of God in me.

We often liken the mind to a computer process of input equals output. This means that you will only get out of the computer what has been put in. We all are born and raised in sin before coming to Christ and there is a lot of garbage that we've acquired since birth. Before Christ I had allowed my body to be a vessel towards sin and now that I was a born again Christian, I had to succumb my body to vigorous exercise and perfect every muscle through training like an athlete.

Like a child I had to go through the stages: I had to learn to sit, then crawl, then stand with the support of structures around me before I started walking perfectly. Transformation is a process of having to unlearn old habits and diligently learn new ones as your mind is being renewed daily. When I felt discomfort to the point of leaving the relationship it was because of who I was becoming in my mind and in my spirit. Bit by bit my mind was conforming to His will and I had to let go of the old in order to embrace the new. I wanted God desperately and I had been taught and was convicted that He dwells in Holy places. If I wanted the Lord as much as I did, then I had to make room and pursue holiness.

This was easier said than done and just the thought brought so much pain in my heart I cried a river. I had loved this man as my friend for years and letting go of him welcomed feelings of a uncertain future for me. I was tempted to string him along, to have in in my life as a friend, but I knew deep down that I would be manipulating the turn of events. You know how we get sometimes: we say we have let go of the steering wheel but we are holding on somewhere "just in case". I also struggled trusting that God could do better than him. Obviously I had yet to know our God!

Eventually I did let go, knowing that God is not mocked. If I wanted Him as much as I said then I should sacrifice that which my heart holds dear. I learned not only to wait on the Lord but to wait right. I learned not only to practice abstinence but to pursue holiness as a lifestyle. I wanted purity that would attract God's presence and I wanted to hand over my life. I understood that it would cost me *everything* , and it did.

I learned that there is so much grace available for us to do God's will once we make a decision to commit to Him wholeheartedly. Pursuing a lifestyle of purity was about more than sex, it was about everything: my thoughts, my words, and my ways had to be submitted to holiness. It was treating every word of God with honour and respect whether people were present or not. It was here that I realised how wicked I am without God's intervention in my life. I was weak and many times He rescued me from my own self. I know without a doubt that had His strength not been made perfect in my times of weakness I would have given to dogs what belonged to the king.

Once I took hold of the grace to finally let go of my flesh's desires, I threw myself into God like one who has nothing else in the whole world. He had chosen me and now I was choosing Him with all of my heart and all of me. The love He reciprocated is unmatched to this day.

I have loved you with an everlasting love; I have drawn you with unfailing kindness. Jeremiah 31:3 (NIV)

He told me this until my whole being claimed and lived it as my truth. In the light of His love I saw a new me coming to light. He took away the shame of my past and cleaned me of my filth. There is no sin that was too big for Him to forgive. He said, "Behold *all* things have passed away." He told me that I was beautiful and wonderfully made and that I was precious in His sight. All the love I yearned for, I found so much more in Him. I was beautiful, complete, forgiven, and bought at a high price. I am royal and I am chosen, this is my identity.

Therefore if any man be in Christ, he is a new creature: old things have passed away; behold, all things are become new.
2 Corinthians 5:17 (KJV)

But you are a chosen people, a royal priesthood, a holy nation, God's special possession, that you may declare the praises of Him who called you out of darkness into His wonderful light. 1 Peter 2:9 (NIV)

I did not want to be a church member anymore, I wanted to get involved with the Father's business in the church and outside the church. I soaked myself in His Word, I read books, I listened to sermons, and attended other church conferences as I felt led to. I acquired knowledge and by the help of the Holy Spirit I received understanding. The more I chased after Him, the more of Him I wanted. I was so hungry for more and more of Him and He met with me. There is truly nothing greater than the Father's love! My prayer is that you will find this love for yourself as you encounter Him in deeper ways. It's the kind of love that marks you for life, you can never remain the same.

Living the dream

I breezed through my first year of university studies. I approached it with the same attitude I did the bridging year – I worked hard and it showed in my results. I was, however, confronted yet again with Mathematics and Physical Science. At first I was terrified because of my history with these two subjects but it became clear at to me that I could not do away with them in the quest for a Bachelor of Pharmacy degree. I made a choice quickly to overcome my fears. It occurred to me that my defeat was, first of all, in my mind, and therefore if I changed my perception about these subjects, I would get different results. This was my theory and I set out to prove it. During lectures I made sure that I engaged my mind fully, listening attentively. After lectures, when I got back to my room, I went over the day's lecture and where I did not understand I went to see the lecturer until I was clear. This worked very well, after a few months I found that I was not struggling anymore.

One thing that remained a struggle that year was the area of finances. My moving around the same mountain had cost my parents a great deal financially. At the time, all four of their children were furthering their studies and my parents were giving every last penny. My experience had taught me to appreciate every cent. I remember the day I asked them to increase my pocket money from R300 to R500. It was a big deal to me until my friend told me that she gets R1000. Wow! I could not believe it! I had learned to live within my means. This meant that I could not afford the latest fashion trends and hairstyles. I refused to look at myself as disadvantaged and this helped me not to fall into temptations.

I saw some people entering into relationships for the benefits of living a certain lifestyle. Even now it is common to see young girls dating older men so that they can be trendy wearing Brazilian weaves. One thing has always been certain, when a man spends on you they expect repayment and in most cases it's with your body. I hated feeling that I owed someone and I resolved that my body would not be used as a means of payment. In order to avoid unnecessary pressures, I cut my hair short and wore it confidently. Where clothes were concerned my best friend helped me a lot. She was from a well-off family and had a better wardrobe than me so whenever I visited her she would give me some of her clothes. I learned to see God in the smallest of things and be grateful for everything.

I recall going to the mall one day to buy groceries and I passed by one of the expensive stores. I decided to go in just to have a look and one particular pair of shoes caught my attention. It was so beautiful and I couldn't resist the urge to try it on. My heart melted. "It looks so good on me and it compliments my legs," I thought. I had to snap back to reality. I took the shoes off but somehow they stayed in my mind.

I remember going back to my residence and convincing myself to forget the shoes. It cost R500! My sister was around at the time and I think I told her about them. She had cooked for us, we ate, and I slept even though it was in the afternoon. When I woke up later I noticed a plastic bag on the table and wondered what it was. I stood up and went to see the plastic bag. "What's this?" I asked my sister. She told me that a friend from church came by to drop it for me. I love gifts and my heart started racing but I had to practice restraint. I slowly opened the plastic bag and saw a shoe box inside from the same fancy store. I wanted to tear the box open but I did not want to assume things. I opened the box and there were the shoes! I looked at my sister puzzled. I asked her to explain in detail what exactly happened. I still couldn't understand so I picked up the phone and dialled my friend. She told me that the Lord put it in her heart to gift me with the shoes. Our good God is into details my dear sisters.

I wore those shoes until they were worn out years later. I fixed them and wore them until I could no longer wear them. They were the most precious pair I had. This taught me a great lesson: God provides and honours those who will choose to honour Him. I was not willing to date for the benefit of fancy shoes, bags, clothes, and a lavish lifestyle. He saw my heart and wanted to give me all that and I wanted to keep my body pure.

During my second year, the Lord blessed me with a bursary that covered me until I completed my studies. It covered school fees and accommodation and I still had extra money to take care of everything else. I could afford all these things that my heart desired. The Lord makes a way, one just needs to make a decision to follow Him wholeheartedly.

Everything seemed to be progressing well in all areas of my life. This is until the third year of my studies. Third year was difficult, even more so because we were anticipating doing our honours degrees the following year. I was still working hard but I think there was a small degree of laxity that almost compromised my journey. When my first semester result came out I received the shocking news. I had failed one module and it was a semester module. The reality was that because it was a semester module I had to wait for the next year to redo it. This meant that the following year I would not be allowed into my final year. I would have to come back and redo that one module and wait for the rest of the year! I was scared. I felt that I had messed up big time. How did I allow myself to fail? I cannot tell you how many times I went to the department pleading that I be allowed to carry this module over whilst I do my last year. "It simply could not be done, it had never been done before," was the response I got. The department made that rule because of the work load in the fourth year. They felt that one would not make it if they carried over any third year modules work. It made sense.

By this time, I regarded myself as strong in the Lord because I had a better understanding of God and certain truths. I decided to reject what I was being told. I recalled that the Lord had promised me that I would finish the degree in four years. Repeating that module for the entire year meant that I would complete the degree in five years and I did not accept that. I was like a mad person, going to the department dean, lecturers, and student unions. They kept telling me that it could not be done. In my closet I was not resting, but waging war in prayer. In faith I was declaring those things that were not as though they were. I would come out of my prayer closet feeling high, so convinced that they would approve my request. The dean already knew me by name and when I went to her office she would not even wait for a greeting. "It can't be done, Jezile," she would say.

You may think I am talking about a few days of fighting. Days passed, months passed, and the year ended. My fear was that the following year January I needed to be in the final year class with my classmates. January came and I was still caught in between. I decided to attend the final year lectures and when the third years were attending this module I would skip fourth year lectures and go and attend with the third years. I really did not care that everyone could see that I was repeating a module, I had my race to run and finish.

January and February passed and I became scared. I was unofficially attending fourth year classes. The duration for the module was three months and I would have to write one test in March. Once I wrote that test it would officially mean that I completed my third year. In March as the test dates were approaching I became aggressive in prayer. This faith thing had to work. If God opened the Red Sea, if He rose from the dead, if He did all those impossible things surely He could do this?! I pressed on, some moments I was full of faith, other moments I was operating on the smallest amount of faith. It had to work.

I recall being called by the dean and thinking, "This woman, what is she going to say now?" I arrived to her office and this time she was smiling. She congratulated me and gave me the letter that allowed me to complete my final year! Yes, this is our God who opens the way where there seems to be no way. He rewrites laws to show favour on His children. He did it for me. It had never been done in our departments history but they did it for me. Glory be to God. I jumped out of that office and met my friend in the corridor. We started praising the Lord out loud right there. I shared with many what the Lord had done for me and many were inspired as God did greater works for them.

Becoming a son

As a person who loves words I inevitably fell in love with the Word of God. As I searched the scriptures I came across words I did not understand and refused to pass them without knowing their meaning. I learned that I belonged to the Kingdom of our God and the word 'kingdom' struck a nerve. I searched and prayed for more understanding. In its meaning I found the purpose to my existence and life changed completely for me. God was equipping me with answers to the two questions every person asks in their lives around identity and purpose.

A kingdom basically is a domain that belongs and is ruled by the king. God created heaven and it became a realm ruled by God as King. The book of Genesis tells us that in the beginning God created the earth and made man in His image and likeness to rule over the earth realm.

So God created mankind in his own image, in the image of God he created them; male and female he created them. God blessed them and said to them, "Be fruitful and increase in number; fill the earth and subdue it. Rule over the fish in the sea and the birds in the sky and over every living creature that moves on the ground."
Genesis 1:27, 28 (NIV)

Earth was an extension of heaven and Adam was appointed as an ambassador of Heaven here on earth. Adam and Eve lived in perfect fellowship with Heaven and executed their responsibilities in the likeness of God. That was until they committed sin by disobeying the command of God. They were deceived by satan and as consequence of their sin were stripped of their power, their authority, and most of all their direct fellowship with God. Since then satan had the stolen power over the earth and mankind has been subject to him.

This was until God sent Jesus Christ, His only Son who is God, to come to earth through virgin birth and be born human like us. Through sin man lost power and authority over the kingdom of earth and it would take a man without sin to restore this authority back to mankind. This is why God did not send an angel or Jesus in His divine form to restore what was lost. God respects and exalts His Word above Himself. So, Jesus being God and human without sin, paid the price and died on the cross to justify through His blood all who would come accepting that He died not for His sins but for theirs, declaring Him as their Lord.

Christ came to establish the Kingdom of Heaven here on earth, to restore all that was lost back to God and back to all who are saved through Him. Above all this He came to restore fellowship and a relationship with God for all.

God taught me to have a kingdom mentality and to stop

living only for myself as if there is no eternity or life after death. To cultivate a kingdom mentality is therefore to live life with this knowledge as foundation and also as one's mindset. To know that you are not of this world, that your citizenship is in heaven. Heaven is our home and we are here as ambassadors of Heaven. This tells us that we have a great responsibility.

So we are Christ's ambassadors; God is making his appeal through us.
We speak for Christ when we plead, "Come back to God!"
2 Corinthians 5:20 (NIV)

As kingdom citizens our mission is to bring souls into the Kingdom of our God and establish the culture of heaven in them. We are to be like Christ in character and allow the Father's business to be our primary occupation. We are visitors on earth; this is not our home. Too many of us become distracted and pay a great deal of attention to earthly things that will not last. We lack greatly when it comes to our God-given assignments.

I learned service

As He taught me these things, a fire was burning inside of me to be a partner in whatever the Lord was doing in our time. I wanted Him to use my voice, my hands, and my feet: all of me. I was driven to serve in many ways, I believed that there is nothing I could not do and whatever I was not skilled at the Lord would enable me to do or bring me human resources. I organised and spoke at women's conferences, teaching and encouraging young people to keep themselves sexually pure. Everywhere I moved to I would ask God to use me. Many times He led me to take young girls and teach them God's word and way of life. I availed myself as a tool in my Master's hand and I saw people's lives being transformed.

The end is near and souls need not only to be brought to God but to become established in God by becoming sons. I have seen satan capitalising on keeping those who are converted in one state, never allowing them to have an actual encounter with God. Eventually he knows that they will walk away and oh how hard it is for those who were once 'saved' to come back to God.

So, as you wait for the realisation of His promises in your life please understand that there is more to salvation than being blessed with a husband or whatever else. Make sure that you join a Bible-teaching church and submit to that leadership. Get involved in the worker's team, remembering that the devil loves idle hands. Quit thinking that you will just sneak in and out of church no matter how great your reasons sound. What seems wise to you may be a way headed for destruction. You are partnering with God and His work when you serve. Do not just wait to be an usher only on Sunday and religiously call that service. Ask God to give you a heart of service. This was the heart of Jesus, He had a mission and He kept Himself in tune with the Father. Whatever He saw the Father doing, that He did as well. When you keep fellowship with God you will be in tune with what He is doing and whatever breaks

His heart will in turn break yours. People who have captured the heart of God and who continue to be in touch with Him will not just sit still unless it is the Lord who tells them to.

I learned to give

When I was a student I surrendered my finances to the Lord. I had a bursary and I told God that I wanted to use some of the money towards serving His people. I had learned to live with an open hand principle, meaning nothing I own is truly mine. God has the right to take all I have, I gave Him those rights. This has allowed me to witness God's heart and hand in ways beyond my imagination. I have given Him priority over my finances to instruct me on how to use them. This does not mean that He tells me when to buy myself a pair of shoes or do my hair, it means that if He leads me to sacrifice doing my hair this month, instead giving to meet someone's need, I do that.

I remember leaving my residential place one afternoon to go to town which was not very far from the university. It was winter and during this season it quickly gets dark outside. I was taking the last taxi back to the university and we were waiting for it to fill up with students. I recall impatiently waiting for the taxi to fill up because the cold was unbearable.

I must have been looking outside the taxi window, hoping to see more students coming to fill the taxi when a strange sight caught my attention. On the pavement next to our taxi I saw young boys, about five of them, sleeping on the floor. Each of them had dirty clothes wrapped around their tiny frames. In disbelief I focused my gaze to study the picture in front of me in more detail. Was there a mattress under their bodies? Were their clothes warm enough? They were sleeping on the floor with no mattress and I was certain that the clothes covering their bodies were not warm enough. I was torn inside because I was freezing inside the taxi. I could not imagine what they were going through.

I wanted to do something and I cried out to the Lord to help me. God did not lead me to taking those boys away from the streets but He led me to an orphanage with younger boys and girls. I 'adopted' those beautiful children and would buy them clothes, blankets, and monthly groceries using the bursary money. I soon realised that what I was getting was not enough and after prayers to God He soon linked me with someone who partnered with me. I continued ministering to those children with the Word and through meeting physical needs from university days until the first few years of my employment.

I also developed an appreciation for the work of God, seeing people leaving behind their degrees to respond to God's call in their lives. The Lord put it in my heart to partner with these ministries financially and with prayers. There was a time when I put someone who was not my child through the first year of their tertiary education because I was led by the Lord. These are just examples of some of the things the Lord led me to do in the waiting season. I do not have millions in my back account but I know and have seen God do things in my life that only He could do. I can always approach Him in boldness whenever I am in need because the Bible says that when we give to the poor we are borrowing to the Lord and God can not owe anyone.

Giving was and still is for me an agreement which I have with God. We always want to receive from God but there comes a time when a child matures into a man in the kingdom and starts delighting in giving instead. The Bible says that it is more blessed to give than to receive. If you to give yourself as a seed to God, I can assure you the returns are immeasurable. When God looks for a man or woman to trust with certain things, it will be you He chooses. By your decision to give of yourself, you would have divinely positioned yourself for certain works and rewards.

When you work with the principles of the Kingdom of God, you learn soon enough that you have to be generous with your time. I remember one year I was invited to be a guest speaker at a youth revival. Going there I had been told I would minister on the Friday but when I arrived I was informed that I was to minister that Saturday morning and evening. I could deal with this as I thought I would spend the night preparing. To my shock these young people started coming to my room for counselling one by one that very night. I was exhausted from having come from another city and needed rest. Soon enough I realised that rest was a luxury that I would not have. I had to give of my time and my body. I'm using the word "body" because it was during this time that I realised that people do not come to you to solve their problems, they come to God in you. Hours passed as I just literally sat there and watched the Holy Spirit minister through me. I managed to sleep just before the sun came up and went in for my session surrendered to God. He took over in one of the ways that I will never forget.

I learned to give my time to God and His dealings. There is a greater reward for this not only in Heaven, but on this side as well. You learn that God holds time in His hand and that whatever we give to Him is invested and not wasted.

As I kept myself busy doing the Father's business a son was born in me! I worked as hard at school to show diligence in all the matters that the Lord had entrusted me with. On the other hand, I never lost sight of whose I was and what I had been called to do. I will never forget my university years; strong foundations were laid that guide me through life even today. I came alive in ways I had never experienced before and I experienced just how beautiful it is to walk with the Lord. I knew very well that I had been marked for life. Four years went by fast and at the end of my fourth year I walked away with a degree in Bachelor of Pharmacy. Faithful God!

The broken heart

In our last year of studying we were required to choose five facilities where we would have prefered to be placed for a Pharmacy internship. It was shocking for me to find out I was placed in a community health center which I had not chosen. I had never heard of the name and I remember going to the computer lab just to google and see where the place was. What I saw grieved me. Everyone else was happy with their placements and I sat there, tears welling up in my eyes. I did not like what I saw, it looked like some small abandoned place. I had to go see the place before moving there the following year, which was just a few months away. I remember feeling that God had abandoned me on the way there. Why would He allow for this to happen?

He told me that it was the people that He was sending me to and promised me that He would be with me. That was enough for me, I had learned that the best life is when you are at the center of God's will. I worked the hardest that year not just as an intern but in fulfilling God's purpose. I breathed serving God and I felt at my best as His presence and joy filled me. I witnessed how God can use anyone as long as we availed ourselves and surrendered our lives to living right before Him. I literally felt a spiritual high if there is such a thing.

It was during this busy period in ministry and career that I met a man at my work place. When we met I knew that He was not a born again Christian and as we continued to talk it was clear in my spirit what my role was: to reconcile Him to God. As the Lord would have it I ceased the opportunity and ministered to him until he gave His life to the Lord and joined a church.. I would pray for him and at times we would pray together.

Soon enough he started showing interest in me and if my memory serves me well it didn't take me that long to fall for him, after all he was in Christ now. As a reader looking in from the outside of the experience you maybe have a better view and insight to see where this went wrong. My heart was already falling for him and so I approached God. What I thought was Him, but was rather my flesh, said that he was the one. I told my pastors about him and he told his.

We were not allowed to be officially engaged until we had met parents and done all that is required by culture. We had gone home and he paid the *lobola*, or bride price, in full. My parents were so happy and so proud of me and I was overjoyed to finally be making them proud of me. Many neighbors attended the event and soon the news spread. I had not fallen back in ministry or in my walk with God and so I believed it was definitely of the Lord. We had our own challenges but you don't look at those as warning signs, just as the enemy fighting what you think God has ordained.

We were supposed to get married at the end of that year and we postponed it. After this I was due to move to another province for work and that meant that we would be about ten hours' drive apart. My spirit kept on hinting that something was not right but I kept rationalising this as my own fears.

When I moved to the new place there was a certainty deep within that this marriage would never take place. The devil is a liar; I would fight in warfare prayers. The following year I felt a drift, he was pulling away and my parents and friends were asking me when the wedding was going to take place. I had no answers. The next four months were torture, I spent every day chasing after shadows. I struggled to get hold of him on the phone and when I did it felt as though there was a wall between us. I was a grown up, I knew he was deliberately creating a rift because to him the relationship was over.

On second thought I rationalised out these thoughts and escaped to what was imaginary, believing he will come back to me and realise that I was the best thing in his life. I was in denial and I did not want my family to know what was really going on. As months progressed I was desperate for answers and so I drove to meet him. That is when he told me that we would not get married – ever. His reasons made sense but the fighter in me just refused. I cried desperately but that did not solve anything. I begged him to stay but that, too, did not work. I went back home to inform my parents; it was the hardest thing. I had brought shame to my family, how would they respond when friends and neighbors asked about the wedding? I was concerned about them but they were concerned about my wellbeing.

At first I was in denial, so I did what any woman would do when her future house seems under threat, I entered warfare. There were times when I literally felt the grace to fight. I wanted back what I believed was mine by force. However, as months passed I started feeling exhausted spiritually, emotionally, and physically. What started off as firing darts during my intense prayer sessions was now replaced by what seemed like empty bullets. A river of tears was replaced by a dry well accompanied by coldness and a distant look from me. There was a time I ended up in hospital because I suffered from severe headaches and could not sleep. I lost a lot of weight and looked skeletal. I still hate pictures taken from that period.

Moving on was the hardest for me because I had imagined the relationship was from God. In my mind I thought of the people who knew about it, the church and the community. In all these places I had raised the banner of Christ and I was ashamed, too embarrassed by what I thought people would say. Too many emotions and feelings of shame came over me. I was convicted of God's existence and therefore did not leave the church but my Bible that was always by my bedside was now collecting dust. I just could not read it; I was disappointed with God. I asked myself too many questions I could not get answers to. Did He not say that He loved me, why would he allow me to go through this shame? Why was the God I had served and loved unreservedly now making a public mockery of me before the very people I had preached the Gospel to? I did not spend time with God as I used to nor did I read the Bible at home. I felt so lost and alone. However, one thing I did not let go off was fellowship with the believers even though I knew that I was not fit to minister to anyone.

I am choosing to open this part of my life because in my walk I have come across many people who walk away from God because they feel He failed to come through, that He disappointed them. There are also those who are convinced that God exists and therefore do not want to go away from God's house irrespective of how they feel. This is good but this, too, can be quite dangerous. God has called us to forever be in His presence and not just His house. How can we truly love and devote ourselves in purity when our heart is not right? A disappointed heart finds it hard to trust, being a testimony of that myself. If He disappointed you before how can you trust that He will carry His other promises? So, yes, some stay in God but their hearts are guarded against Him.

Not looking to your own interests but each of you to the interests of the others. In your relationships with one another, have the same mindset as Christ Jesus:

Who, being in very nature God, did not consider equality with God something to be used to his own advantage; rather, he made himself nothing by taking the very nature of a servant, being made in human likeness. And being found in appearance as a man, he humbled himself by becoming obedient to death – even death on a cross! *Philippians 2:4-8 (NIV)*

The first truth that liberated me was God taking me to the root of Christianity. God so loved us that He gave His beloved Son, His only Son to die for us. Jesus Christ did not think much of Himself as God but faced the shame on the cross. He allowed the Father to publicly humiliate Him in front of His enemies and by the same people whom He ministered to, healing them of their disease. He knew no sin but in order to reconcile us to God the Father, He had to be sin for us by taking all our sins and carrying them on Himself. During that hard season in my life I was asking how He could put me to shame so publicly. Who am I in the light of what Christ went through? Who was I to seek to preserve my image when Jesus Christ disregarded His position of glory because of my iniquities? When we go through these feelings may God teach us humility lest we exalt ourselves and our positions above or as equals to God.

I went around this mountain for months, unable to hear God speaking until one day I heard Him saying, "Andiswa, you moved ahead of me!" Imagine, moving ahead of God and not walking in partnership with Him by following His lead every step of the way. He was there at the beginning and had made it clear to me why this man was in my life. My flesh had taken over and I wanted to eat from the vineyard that I was to look for in God. The beginning of a matter usually holds clarity in the vision going ahead but sometimes we want what we want. If we had gotten married it would not have been the will of God and my lust would have caused abortion of many things in both our lives.

It is the most fertile, yet dangerous, ground to be disappointed with God. This soil is fertile enough for the enemy to start planting seeds of doubt and distrust in God, and even worse, making you to question the existence of God. It is during this state of mind that you might be introduced to other religions and because you have left your safe zone it might just be easy to be bought out of Christianity. Most people who have denounced God have done so because they were disappointed by Him. If you are to go the long run in God you must live by principle, let God be true to every man, including yourself.

Not at all! Let God be true, and every human being a liar. As it is written: "So that you may be proved right when you speak and prevail when you judge." Romans 3:4 (NIV)

God is always right, He never lies, and what He promises He will always do. So, when you are tempted to feel that He has disappointed you, start to evaluate and get a better perspective. Sometimes God says, "Not now my son/daughter." At times He is saying, "This is not best for you and as a Father I ask that you would trust me with your heart and life and let go so I can work out the best plan for you." In my case He was telling me to take a step back so that He can lead and take this to where He intended for it to be but I failed to listen and ended up hurt. Do a proper evaluation and I guarantee you that if you are honest you are the one, not God, who missed a step.

If you have been hurt in the waiting season, even by lies and deception of those within the church, I advise you to go to God. Do not walk away from Him or from fellowship with fellow believers. Look out for those the Lord will bring your way carrying the healing balm in their words or companionship. I can honestly say that God may have seemed far but He was not. It was my hardened heart that did not trust Him anymore. My heart was closed and I couldn't see God in my family as they surrounded me with love and support, I couldn't see Him in the new people that came to shower me with kindness. Now as I look back I know and can say, "God, You were there every step of the way." He heals and comforts the broken-hearted as you continue to look and cry to Him. He is your Father and you are the apple of His eye. There is hope and light that beckons if only you look up.

Discovering my identity

"Who am I?" I had battled with this question for the longest time in my life. I still remember having many conversations with my best friend, Samela, trying to unpack this question that clearly had more to it. Its reality seemed to carry a promise of confidence and stability. My best friend would joke about how my answer to "Who am I?" seemed to change each time we met. She was right, even though at the time it scared me to think that I was struggling to know who I was. Somehow it seemed to be tied to finding out why I was here on earth, what my purpose was.

It is only God who holds the right to tell me who I am and why He created me. Unfortunately, many adopt identities that have been given to them by the people and circumstances of life. The Lord heard my cry and addressed this area in my life and since then I have to continue to remind myself. In writing this part allow me to borrow from a blog I wrote a few years back. The experience was real and it has since had a major impact on my identity in Christ and I hope it will have the same impact on you. You may feel that I'm preaching here but my intention is to share with you what I was taught and as I was taught hoping that you will receive the same impact I did.

It was an eventful night with so much thunder and lightning that I found it hard to sleep. The following morning, I received a phone call from a doctor friend who asked me to come and have a look at something and so I went to the maternity ward hurriedly. It was a new-born baby wrapped in a hospital blue cloth. They kept him in an incubator to keep him at an appropriate temperature for survival. I looked at my friend in confusion and asked what had happened. Apparently during the stormy night, the mother had given birth, put the child in a bin bag, and threw him away into the garbage. Somebody found the child and that is how he ended up at the hospital.

I could not hold back the tears as I stared at his frail body in disbelief. It was a baby boy and as I held him I could still see residue of blood on his tiny body. I wondered almost in disgust who would throw away a human being. My heart was so moved by the little creature, I prayed for him. I knew without a doubt that his rough beginnings here on this earth would not determine his life nor his end.

I knew there was a great destiny already on his life and I prayed that God would guide his footsteps and that he would live in that greatness. The nurses suggested I adopt him and I gave it some serious thought. Many things were not in place in my life to raise a child but what determined my decision not to take him was a lesson that the Lord gave me on sonship. This also impacted my life as it introduced me to my own identity in Christ and since then my eyes have been open to the greatest gift and inheritance given to us. Let me share the lesson with you.

The soil we were born to die in

I passed by you and saw you kicking around helplessly in your blood. I said to you as you lay there in your blood, "Live!" I said to you as you lay there in your blood, "Live!" Ezekiel 16:6 (NET)

We were all born into sin by inheritance because of our first parents, Adam and Eve. If sin were represented by blood it would be safe to say that we were swimming in a pool of blood and like that little boy we lay helplessly because we could not save ourselves. Unless somebody came to save him, give or take a few hours, he would have suffocated to death. We, too, were looking at death in the face until Christ came and took our place by taking the wage of death upon Himself. He took what was a penalty due to us so that those who believed in Him would be saved. Salvation by Christ is the most powerful, selfless act of redemption that continues to alter a person's life. It is essential that the package of His death is fully understood so that liberation may occur.

We are Transplanted

Giving thanks to the Father, who has qualified you to share in the inheritance of the saints in light. He has delivered us from the domain

of darkness and transferred us to the kingdom of his beloved Son.
Colossians 1:12 (NIV)

Whosoever believes that Jesus is Lord, that He died on the cross to pay the debt of our sins, and on the third day rose in victory, receives the gift of salvation. Salvation means being delivered from the world we were born into that is ruled by the power of darkness. The Bible tells us that we were transferred into the Kingdom of God. When you have seen a plant being transplanted from one bed of soil to another you will know that the whole plant with its roots is uprooted and planted in the new soil that will allow growth. This is the same thing that happens in salvation; we were in bad soil that caused us to produce bad fruit which led to death as our destiny. When we accept His proposal for salvation of our souls the Father then uproots us. He takes us as we are, with all the garbage that we come with from the past, and plants us anew in His fertile ground. It is as though He is saying, "I recognise My good image in you and that due to the condition of your birth you failed to produce after Me, therefore I want you to come as you are so that I can put you in soil which will cause you to produce in My likeness".

When we are in Christ we become a new creation and day by day in His Word and Spirit we become like Him in our ways.

Therefore, if anyone is in Christ, the new creation has come: The old has gone, the new is here! 2 Corinthians 5:17 (NIV)

We are in grafted

If some of the branches have been broken off, and you, though a wild olive shoot, have been grafted in among the others and now share in the nourishing sap from the olive root ... Romans 11:17(NIV)

Grafting is the practice of joining two plants together permanently, so that they will continue growing as a single organism. Both transplanting and grafting drive the same point home. We received mercy and were adopted into a new home, that of God's. Some branches were removed from the tree due to unbelief and by grace an invitation was sent to us by means of the cross so that when we believe in God, we, the branches, shall be cut from the rebellious tree and be grafted into a new tree. A oneness will happen and we will feed from the nutrients provided to us by the root, which is Christ. When we are saved we become one with God by His Spirit dwelling in us and we are led to walk in likeness to Him both in character and way of life. As we grow in Christ we feed on His nature and with time we become like Him. We become partakers of the promises that were made to Abraham and his descendants and we grow with them as a single organism in Christ. This means that whatever was promised to Abraham is now by position ours as well.

We are adopted as sons

God decided in advance to adopt us into his own family by bringing us to himself through Jesus Christ. This is what he wanted to do, and it gave him great pleasure. Ephesians 1:5 (NIV)

When you adopt a child, you give them a name which becomes an identity. As a Jezile, my maiden surname, I would have given that boy my surname and by virtue of that he would qualify for whatever I have because he would be my son. I would not just provide a roof over his head, food, and clothing – even a servant qualifies for such privileges. Adoption would include my name, my culture, and all that is mine to be given to another who would otherwise not qualify to have them. Whatever I have would automatically belong to that child and he would bear my surname and benefit from all the privileges of being my child. If I give birth to other children, they partake equally of all I have, even of the love I give. This is true adoption. Many have suffered greatly in life because they lacked this knowledge in God.

Yet to all who did receive him, to those who believed in his name, he gave the right to become children of God. John 1:12(NIV)

But when the set time had fully come, God sent his Son, born of a woman, born under the law, to redeem those under the law, that we might receive adoption to sonship. Because you are his sons, God sent the Spirit of his Son into our hearts, the Spirit who calls out, "Abba, Father." So you are no longer a slave, but God's child; and since you are his child, God has made you also an heir. Galatians 4:7(NIV)

So, this is the truth of the Gospel in all its beauty. We are the adopted sons and Christ is the first born in our family. By virtue of adoption God is our Father and we are no longer slaves, servants, or strangers, but His beloved sons whom He bought at the highest price. As His sons, we have everything that is our Fathers and that is everything! The earth is the Lord's and all that is therein belongs to God and He gave it to Christ and we are co-heirs with Christ.

This is the beauty of salvation, a whole new world whose truth is worth believing and living in. His Spirit in us is our DNA that proves again and again that we are of God and, like our Father, we are royal. It is time we walked in the light of this truth, it is time that we learned the culture we have been adopted into. We are the sons of grace, we once looked at ourselves and knew that we were not worthy of this royal crown. We were hopeless and death was a guarantee that looked back at us. No good deeds could ever merit us this royal name. The more we tried to be right with God the deeper we sunk into darkness. Yet, God looked at us. He did not just look through us by focusing on our fallen, broken, and filthy state and disqualifying us like many did. The stench of our sin did not keep God away in disgust but His love drew Him to partake of our stench as He drew us out. He who was without sin became sin for us, dying on the cross in our place. This is so that we could become sons of God.

As I learned this truth and made it my truth, it set me free.

This is who I am, this is who you are! I started allowing this truth to affect me and every area of my life. I started witnessing how bold I was becoming and the way I looked at life changed completely. I was still waiting on God for marriage to the right partner but this occupied my entire existence. I was loving and claiming my identity.

Maybe you have not heard about this and maybe you have but you have not lived in its profound reality. I invite you to partake of your heritage. It will allow you to overcome feelings of inadequacy and of walking around like a victim of circumstances. Knowing who you are in Christ will set you apart and give you the confidence to live a victorious life.

I know that I am the daughter of a King, loved with no bounds and highly favoured. I am wonderfully made and set apart for great works. I am who God says I am and I have all that He says I have in Christ. I am royalty.

The ties that bind us

It felt like the most beautiful setting filled with people and the atmosphere bursting with anticipation. I wasn't so much aware of his physical appearance more than his presence right there before me. He knelt down and right then I became aware that it was a ring he was holding in his hand. My heart paced fast and I knew then that the answer to his question was at the tip of my tongue. I was impatiently waiting for those words, "Will you marry me?" to blurt out a resounding, "Yes!" Just as I was about to accept the proposal I was distracted by someone who suddenly appeared right beside me. It was not just his presence that distracted everyone but the fact that the strange man wrapped one of his hands around my waist. Before I could protest he spoke in the most authoritative and possessive voice, "Back off, she's my wife," speaking to the almost fiancé. The moment was so intense and definite one could hear the sound of a pin falling to the ground. I was so angry and felt captive to this man's accusations!

I woke up from the dream with a sickening feeling in my stomach. My heart was deeply hurt and for a moment I struggled to breathe. "Thank you Jesus it was a dream, thank you Lord."

I uttered these words repeatedly as though to actually convince myself that this was just a dream. My heart weighed heavy, my spirit seemed grieved. I had had such feelings before and I knew that the only way was to pray and seek meaning from the Lord. I prayed and cancelled any hindrances of the enemy on my future marriage. I felt lighter after prayer but my mind could not let go of the dream. I had hit thirty years already and still the man I was waiting for was nowhere to be found.

There were moments were my hopes were high and my faith unshakable but other moments were lonely. During these low moments I felt alone despite many activities and people around me. I would come back from work and head straight for the bedroom. If only I could just sleep away the creeping pain. Sometimes sleep would help and sometimes I would wake up to the same reality. Had God forgotten about me? He said that He loved me and I had served Him with all that I am, but why did it feel like He had His back to me? People who had just gotten saved were getting married faster than me and I wondered if maybe there was something I was not getting right. It seemed it was easier for people outside Christianity. They received everything they wanted at the snap of their fingers and I had to wait so long for the same things. I knew that I could never walk away from Him; I locked that door behind and threw away the key.

This dream was improper and the timing was imperfect. I pondered long and when I felt the heavy weight upon me I called my spiritual mentor. For the longest time in my life I had prayed for a mentor but God closed that door. It was almost two years after the broken engagement that this door opened when I least expected it. I witnessed my mentor labouring hard over me. I saw God using a surrendered married man and his family to meet with me in such a raw and profound manner. God used him to uproot every confusion, heal my brokenness, and teach me His ways. It was like heaven opened up its floodgates and poured a rain of restoration over me.

I saw God attending to my every case through him. He answered questions I was too afraid to ask. Above all I was confronted by such immense love of the Father. Often my mind would raise the question, "What manner of love is this?" I was blown away by God, His grace, and love. My early beginnings in Christianity were founded on God's love that had amazed me. I often say that I am a child of love, I craved for it growing up, it found me in early youth, and it shapes me to this day. If you do not have someone walking closely with you, who is older and more mature spiritually, and who lives to testify of God, please pray for one. God has various means of doing this and sometimes it could be various people who help shape our lives, some who we may not have met physically. When we walk with the wise, we become wise.

As I was saying, I called my mentor after this dream. After much prayer and counsel, the issue of my previous engagement came up again. For the longest time this topic was forbidden because of the pain it still brought. However, I had received healing, praise be to God, and I was willing to confront it.

Tradition and the Bible show us the significance of the shedding of blood. Agreements and covenants were sealed by shedding blood. My engagement had gone beyond just the putting of a ring on the finger. Both families had met and *lobola* was paid with slaughtering of sheep afterwards. The families were in agreement and the wedding date had been set. The engagement was broken about a month before the wedding. In many cultures this means that the two are husband and wife and anything is permissible, meaning that they can also make children. This is so in our culture. In Christianity, however, the process does not mean marriage. A marriage is at the consent of both parents, being joined together in the presence of witnesses by an ordained man of God, followed by consummation through sexual intercourse. In my case as a Christian then, I was not married yet.

The dream did bring into attention the detail of *lobola* which was still in my father's house. My ex refused to come and collect it and this had many implications. As a Christian I had to pay back what belonged to him. This was vital because for as long as this was not done it seemed to have left a connection between us. I was free from him but deep down I knew the tie was still there. I thought that time would let this fade away but what I did not know was that a lot more needed to be undone spiritually to break free physically. I remember the day his *lobola* was returned, the relief that came from within. Words were spoken to undo all that was done, I prayed also to renounce all spiritual accusations. Walking away brought a new meaning and respect from both of us. It literally felt like I had been given a new clean heart, to see him purely with no reminder of the past whatsoever. Only God is able to that, such perfect and complete work!

This brings me to what we call soul mates. Society has taught us from a young age to pursue the ideal of a fairytale. We grow up marveling at those of the opposite sex we perceive to have found a connection with. We pursue it for our own fulfilment, the love of a lifetime. Apparently it happens only once so we meet someone and, blinded by our own desires, are drawn by chemistry and bind ourselves to them. We think this love will last and when it breaks we are broken. Before too long this same chemistry develops with another and so the cycle continues. Our heart breaks and we use various means to get over a broken heart. We are mostly not aware of the damage that these soul ties cause us. Such ungodly ties do not just disappear over time or when we get married or fall in love with someone else. We have all heard stories of people who were married and then one day they bump into an ex-boyfriend or girlfriend. After a few instances of exchange in conversation they find themselves alone and the inevitable happens.

The soul is the core for passions, desires, love, hate, and all the appetites of the body. It is a sphere of our emotions, affections, our will, and intellect. Having our souls tied to somebody in an ungodly manner fragments the soul, and is destructive. When we walk away we are prone to feeling bound to them, having emotional and sexual longings for them. Some people have tended towards self-destruction, even attempting suicide once these relationships end.

And Dinah, the daughter of Leah, which she gave birth unto Jacob, went out to see the daughters of the land. And when Shechem, the son of Hamor the Hivite, prince of the country, saw her, he took her and lay with her and defiled her. And his soul was joined unto Dinah, the daughter of Jacob, and he fell in love with the damsel and spoke unto her heart. Genesis 34:2-3 (Jubilee Bible 2000)

Their souls were fastened or glued together. This joining together, or oneness, was designed by God to happen between a male and a female who are married. A violation of this has consequences. My pastor once illustrated soul ties in this way: he took pages of white, red, and yellow paper and glue. He said that each page represents an individual's soul before forming ties with anyone. He then took the white sheet and glued it to the red sheet. After a few minutes he tried to separate she sheets and we could see that each sheet was no longer in its pure form but had been torn in some areas and had on it pieces of the other colour. He then took this paper that now had white and red and glued it to the clean yellow paper. He followed the same step. At the end the yellow paper had white and red pieces on it. This is how each of us are in our souls, connections with this one and that one. Pieces of us here and there. Yet, we keep going, feeling empty somehow and expecting someone else to fill this void. Marriage is not an institution for filling voids. It takes two complete individuals to enjoy quality marriage.

That dream brought this to my attention. We develop and harness these unhealthy ties through sexual intimacy, making vows of "I will love you forever," "I will never be with another," and also giving symbolic gifts that mark our bond. In preparation for marriage and just to reach a point of fullness as an individual I had to sit down and break the ties to my past. God used this activity to free me from the ties to the past and I would like to share the steps with you. I would like to highlight that this is to be taken very seriously and that means putting aside time, at least a day, to deal with breaking soul ties in your life.

The steps I took in breaking soul ties in my life:

- In the presence of God write down the sins that you have committed and repent of them to God (sex, fondling, shedding blood, etc).

- Think of vows or commitments that you made towards the one you have a soul ties with. Words are powerful and the power of life and death is in the tongue. Repent and renounce these in the name of Jesus Christ.

- Gifts are often given as a symbol of the connection and every time you look at that gift your heart responds and you remember. Gifts like rings, necklaces, underwear, etc are monuments of an ungodly relationship. These have to be thrown away or given away, including pictures and letters.

- This process can bring back pain and resentment. That's why next you need to mention their names and say that you forgive them if you still hold anything against them.

- The next step is to verbally break the soul ties:

"In Jesus' name, I renounce any ungodly soul tie that was formed between myself and _____ as a result of _____ (fornication, etc.)."

- The bible says that whatsoever we bind on earth is bound in heaven and whatever we lose is loosened. This is the heritage of the children of God. Use this time to thank God for forgiveness of sins, for healing, and for victory.

Congratulations, know that he whom the Son Jesus Christ sets free is free in deed. Go in this truth and see the transformation.

The skeletons in the Closet

The issue of being settled in marriage never left people's lips. There is a tendency to wear this status with shame, especially in some gatherings. Parents can lose patience with your status and your married friends' concern can make you feel worse rather than hopeful. I remember this doctor friend of mine calling me out of the blue and telling me to be careful of delaying marriage and risk giving birth to children with birth defects. I was heartbroken and angry at the same time. I felt she was insensitive and I had reminded myself that it wasn't that there was no man interested in marrying me; I was waiting on God to direct me to the one He most preferred for me.

Really now, can people please practice sensitivity when approaching these areas? The truth is that we do want to get married, we are worried just like everybody else. We have moments when we are optimistic and then the next moment we are tempted to ask God, "Why me?" Instead of asking us questions we have no answers for, why not redirect things to God who holds time in His hand. Praying for people in their season of waiting would help in a tremendous way.

Friends were getting married and bearing children and silently I wondered if I would ever be blessed like that. Would I even be able to bear children once I got married? A silent fear would creep in and I would declare the promises of God that none of His children would be barren. I learned that during these vulnerable times I was most prone to sin in some way and this is where accountability matters. I was blessed with spiritually mature people around me who would keep checking up on me and sometimes I would call to chat with them until I did not feel alone any more.

I will never forget the festive season starting at the beginning of December every year. As much as this time is about Christmas and family, there was just something about it that maximised my lonely feelings. I hated going to the malls at this season. You look around and *everybody* seems to be holding hands with their lover. Or was it just me focusing on things my heart was longing for?

I recall one day driving to the mall and, just before leaving my car, seeing so many couples passing by and I could not leave the car. I just sat inside the car and observed as an outsider. I longed for love, I longed to hold somebody's hand and to look into their eyes as we laugh at sweet nothings, oblivious to the human traffic at the mall during the festive season. I was alone in the car and I felt vulnerable. A call came, from some man whose name I don't even recall. I wasn't foolish, I knew the great opportunist, the devil, was making me his prey. Liar!

He was going to go hungry that day where I was concerned. I told the guy off and quickly dialed my mentor. I explained to him how I was feeling and exactly where I was.

Accountability is something deep. It allows you to be vulnerable in front of someone else. In my language we say *"Impundu zingaphandle,"* your bums are out. It means that you allow yourself to be honest and transparent, to expose even that thing that has the potential to humiliate you. This is how far we go in pursuit of purity and Christ. My mentor still reminds me of that day and we have a good laugh about it. He calls it my "dustbin moment" and I have a few of those.

During these low moments it is important to keep in touch with the people you are accountable to. Visiting them and their families will help a lot to keep your thoughts in line. Being alone when you are feeling weak or hanging out with people who won't hold you accountable for stepping out of line is accepting the invitation to sin. I knew what my weak areas were and diligently guarded against them.

Temptations to compromise and settle for anyone who mentioned the "M" word never seemed to end. I know too many people who are in this position right now and some have yielded to the temptation and dated a man who led them down the route of compromise. The once zealous for the Lord slowly taking bites of the forbidden fruit and becoming spiritually dull as a result. Singlehood can be a bed for all kinds of temptations and if we are not careful we find ourselves having indulged in sin that we later cover up so that the world doesn't see. In this moment we forget that God sees.

If we were to open the files of singles during their waiting season we would see how the enemy has played on so many, drawing them away from God with lies that look like the truth. Sexual sins are rampant in this season: masturbation, pornography addictions, one night stands, sex with the same sex, and co-habiting – to name just a few. Somehow these sins have become an acceptable struggle, "God knows my weakness and His grace will cover me."

We cannot remain in sin and say grace will abound, it is a lie from the enemy. This is an area where many of us fall. We have made for ourselves an image of who God is and he is very understanding. We engage in sexual activities and make a home in our beds with someone we are not married to. As long as we still go to church on Sunday and put out posts on social media about God's material blessings then we are still good with God. This God understands our weaknesses and we regard anyone who corrects us as judgmental. God cannot be inconsistent, the weapon of the enemy in our generation is appealing to our senses and blurring the image of the true God. Our generation's Christianity preaches receiving from God and nothing about the price payed for being a follower of Christ, or sacrifice. It preaches nothing about denial and fruits of the Holy Spirit. We publicly declare the Word of God only in part and it's those verses that massage our egos and seem to condone our sinful behaviors. We have only brought the measure of Christianity down to financial prosperity and this is utter deception. If I am prospering financially, owning properties, cars, and going to Dubai , New York, and Seychelles for holidays then I am a good Christian who is favored above the rest.

Coming to skeletons in the closet, we have all heard of or even know someone who is suffering from conditions such as heart attacks and strokes. Clogged arteries increase the likelihood of heart attacks, strokes, and even death. Arteries are blood vessels that carry blood rich in oxygen throughout your body. They go to your brain as well as to the tips of your toes. Healthy arteries have smooth inner walls and this allows blood to flow easily through them. Some people, however, develop clogged arteries. Clogged arteries result from a buildup of a substance called plaque on the inner walls of the arteries. This plaque can reduce blood flow, or, in some instances, block it altogether.

Sin is to our spiritual man what plagues are to the flow of blood to the heart. The piling up of sins that one does not confess and turn away from becomes like a plague that clogs the pathway of our communication with God. God requires that we be holy and blameless just as He is because this is the state that allows free flow of fellowship between us and Him.

There is nothing that gives room to the enemy like hidden sins. You know how we fall into temptation and instead of running to God asking for forgiveness and cleansing, we hide the sin in our closets and pretend like it never happened. The thing about sin that is not confessed is that not only does it haunt you, but it has a tendency to repeat itself. It may be hidden to the rest of the world but its effects will spill over to other areas of your life.

So, because it doesn't show we therefore keep on piling up that closet with skeletons until you realise one day how far away from God you have gone. The communion that you once enjoyed with God has been blocked by sin. We have so mastered Christianese, speaking the right words and doing the acts of someone who has been saved but our spirit man is no longer alive in God. Sometimes we are bold enough to continue ministering on the pulpit and act like all is well but deep down we know we sound like empty gongs. We then try too hard to compensate for the anointing we have lost by over performing in worship, prayer, preaching, and every other thing. We know that things are not ok, far from it.

For God's gifts and his call are irrevocable. Romans 11:29 (NIV)

God's gifts unto us are without repentance, He never recalls them or takes them back for any reason, not even our sins. That means they are free and not given to us when we are good people then taken away the moment we sin. This has led many to neglecting their inner man and overcompensating on the exterior as a cover up. As long as I still do the things that make me look like a Christian, I'm good even though I keep ignoring the promptings of the Holy Spirit telling me to come back. The Christian walk is a personal walk with the Lord but somehow we make it about other people. The gifts that God has given us are for the equipping of the saints for the work of service, to the building up of the body of Christ (Ephesians 4:12). It is absolute selfishness and being void of love for God when we continue to minister to people whilst we remain in sin. We may still have the gifts but the one thing that the Lord will take away is His presence.

Sometimes we feel stuck because of the sin that we committed, not knowing if God can still accept us. There was a time when I felt so lost and I did not know how to get back to God. You know that feeling that our sin is too big for God to forgive? Sometimes when I dared look at myself I felt unworthy because I felt disqualified by other Christians. The tendency is to use the same measure to predict how God sees us. This has made many of us to remain in the pits we dug ourselves, feeling that there is no hope and no way back to God. This is a strategy from the enemy; God has provided a permanent way back no matter how red our sins maybe. Christ on the cross, His death, His resurrection, and His blood are the irrevocable testaments of a way back to God no matter how fallen one may be.

I had to practice consciously living a life where God is my only audience, seeking to glorify Him publicly and privately. I had to realise that this walk is about me and God before it is about other people. Having a personal walk perspective tends to bring clarity and a more inward maturing of an individual. It moves from performance-based Christianity to being a son/daughter in the kingdom of our God. It does not matter how far you think you have fallen, there is no such thing with God as a place of no return as long as you still have breath. If this is you, knowing that you have sinned against God and feeling that there is no way back, recognise this moment that God is calling for you. There is nothing that you have done that God has not seen before and made a way of forgiveness for.

Learning repentance

Repentance requires that we come to God and agree to acknowledge that we have sinned before God, and then intentionally leaving that sin at the alter before God and doing a 180 degree turn in the opposite direction. This means that we leave it there and cut ties with whatever tempts you towards that sin. You might have to do some spring cleaning like keeping a distance with some friends or the man/woman of your weakness, to stop watching those movies, or letting go of the object of your attraction. This step has to be deliberate otherwise you may just find yourself back where you started off. I do not intend to preach a doctrine of do's and don'ts but these have gone a long way in keeping one within God's way.

Next one needs to intentionally flee towards the Word of God. I know how much we love our freedom and how we hate being religious but you know what? Sometimes you need to be religious about what keeps your purity intact. Studying the Word of God religiously as though you were indulging in your favorite chocolate is *key* to staying free. Christ is the Word of God and when we study the Word we partake of Christ, of cleansing, and being made to be like Him.

Furthermore, keep yourself occupied. The devil loves idle hands and a void heart and he will do whatever it takes to draw you back to his ways and out of God's plan. It is good that you have confessed your sin and have been forgiven. It is great to be given a new slate to start over but make sure that your house is not empty, fill it up with the Word of God and occupy yourself with things that bring the awareness of God in your life.

When an impure spirit comes out of a person, it goes through arid places seeking rest and does not find it. Then it says, "I will return to the house I left." When it arrives, it finds the house swept clean and put in order. Then it goes and takes seven other spirits more wicked than itself, and they go in and live there. And the final condition of that person is worse than the first. Luke 11:24-26 (NIV)

Lastly, commit to the habit of running to God in humility like David did whenever you fall into sin. David never basked in sin whenever God convicted Him of sin, he ran to God. Do not allow satan to cause you to overlook sin, thinking it is too small compared to what others have done, it's a trap. Sin is sin and it's an offence to God who paid a high price to deliver us from its hold. Confess to God and confess to one another, even though this may be hard if many have taken our confessions and turned them into the latest gossip. Pray to God to lead you to someone you can account to, there is such liberty that comes from letting it all out to someone who will pray with you and cover you in love.

Whoever conceals their sins does not prosper, but the one who confesses and renounces them finds mercy. (Proverbs 28:13) (NIV)

The efforts of my flesh

There are many ways by which the Lord communicates with us and one of those is through dreams. This certainly has been true for me but I must also add that for the longest time I ignored dreams. It would only shock me when I started seeing some things coming to pass. The Bible tells us that dreams can come from much activity during the day and this means that not all dreams have meaning. I have learned not to ignore dreams but to pray about them immediately after waking up. Sometimes I document them and at times I seek counsel on those I can't get immediate interpretation on. Through dreams the Lord has given me promises, warnings, and even rebuked me a number of times.

One day as I was sleeping and I woke up from a dream that felt so real. In this dream I saw angels with wings for the first time and they were walking beside me. The dream was so vivid that I could feel the effect of their presence, maybe because they were so tall with strong bodies. I was fascinated by the whole scene like a child. One of them came close to me and I noticed the long black hair. I couldn't help asking with beaming eyes, "Where is angel Michael?" The angel did not respond but simply smiled and told me that God had heard my prayers and had sent them in response to the prayer. I was so excited to hear this and then the angel moved closer to me as if to whisper something in my ear. The angel spoke about a move that I would make and then for some reason I struggled to hear the rest of what was said.

When I woke up from the dream I was so excited about the promise and the assurance that the Lord had given me. Feelings of relief and gratitude came over me. Finally, after all these years the Lord was fulfilling His promise. I was bothered about the part that was whispered to me which I could not recall. It sounded like a warning and even thinking about it brought the feeling of caution to me. I quickly shoved it aside and lived in this moment of a promise being fulfilled at last.

Days, weeks, and months passed and nothing new came. I still had the same experiences of men outside the Christian faith showing interest in me and those who were Christians I let go of because there was no agreement in my spirit. Hope deferred in deed makes the heart grow sick. I soon regressed to the state of wondering if it had been God who spoke or if it was just my wild imagination. On other days I thought that maybe I did hear from the Lord, maybe I just needed to be more open. I started thinking that maybe the man I'd been waiting for had been under my nose the whole time, isn't that what they often say? Or maybe I already turned him down. All these thoughts made me to follow my soul's desire instead of following the

Spirit's leading. I left my state of resting in God without even knowing it and started rationalising things in my head. Could it be this one or that one? I had left my resting place in Him and had taken over the steering wheel.

This is where most of us are prone to making mistakes. Temptations to open old doors, revisiting the past, and re-igniting an old love will come to play. I was also tempted to rekindle an old flame, thinking that maybe this one was the one, maybe God wants to reconnect us because the right time had come. This is hardly the case, we are just being driven by our own desires and we have actually dethroned God and are now are sitting on that seat of authority, ordering the steps of our lives. This will lead to confusion, heart break, and even delays to getting where God wants you to be. It is a setback.

Then there are those times when we fall for someone who demonstrates some form of godliness but is not a born again Christian. Most of them go to church and this is how they can catch the restless sister/brother on the lookout for "the one". They are kind and caring and seem to meet what our hearts yearn for in terms of the ideal person. They just seem perfect, they say the right things, and massage our egos. The shock comes when we establish that they are actually not really Christian. At this point we have already convinced ourselves that they are good enough and gotten our hearts attached to the idea that they could be "it". Only they are not.

The Bible is clear that we cannot be unequally yoked and this is not God being cruel towards us as it often seems. The idea of being unequally yoked is borrowed from farming. During ploughing season, for tilling of the ground and planting two oxen or other animals are used. They use a yoke to pair oxen together to enable them to pull a load together. This yoke is usually tied around the neck and so these paired animals would go around the entire field carrying the load. It would be dangerous to pair an unfit ox with a strong one, the work might not even get done.

It's the same thing in Christianity. The institution of marriage is sacred and very delicate. We were all sinners before coming to God, this means that we belonged to the kingdom of darkness that is governed by satan. We served him when we lived lives that were ruled by flesh and, even if we wanted to please God, we were not capable of doing so outside Christ. Thank God for Jesus who bought us with a high price, that of His life crucified to death on the cross. Anyone who believes that He died for their sins and follows Him is then transferred from the kingdom of darkness to the kingdom of light. We have spoken about the impact of becoming one which is what inevitably happens in marriage. The Bible poses a question: "What does darkness have to do with light?"

Do you not know that he who unites himself with a prostitute is one with her in body? For it is said, "The two will become one flesh."
1 Corinthians 6:16 (NIV)

Unequal yoking is then the mating of someone who belongs to the kingdom of light with one who belongs to the kingdom of darkness. This is outside the will of God and therefore it is sin. Nevertheless, we are tempted to go ahead and disobey God, giving excuses and rewriting our own doctrine along the way in an effort to justify our actions. "Maybe God wants me to change him, to convert him." That is a lie from the enemy! We do not convert anybody; it is God who brings a lost soul to Christ. It's a trap from the enemy. If we are being honest we can see it when we take that route or by closely watching someone who has. There is a decline spiritually. Those once committed to the things of Gods suddenly find reasons to stay away. They suddenly have issues with one area of the Bible or the leadership. Once isolated, the enemy takes over and sin becomes inevitable.

I had many of these temptations but thank the Lord for His hand that never let go. At the end I realised that the Lord had given a promise and a warning. I cannot attain spiritual things by using the flesh. I learned about me and my own weaknesses, what sins I was most prone to fall in. I then put in place strategies to avoid falling into obvious sins. I learned to love my brothers in the Lord enough not to lead them on when I knew that the Lord has not said so.

In this journey I have learned obedience and discipline. I have learned to love the Lord more than I love myself and to esteem His law. I have also learned to discipline my appetite, to subject my body to obey God no matter what. The training never stops but I have resolved to live life at the center of God's will. This comes with a lot of sacrifices, having to prefer others above yourself. I am still learning to love myself as the Lord loves me and believe His promises for me. Even though some promises still linger, I trust Him.

The idols in my heart

One of the things that I went through as I waited for the man the Lord preferred for me to be married to was dealing with the issue of idols. I remember clearly when the Lord spoke to me, saying, "Remove the idols in your heart." Idols! Me? I almost jumped off my chair. I am Your child, Lord, I do not worship idols. I forsook my background of ancestral worship as soon as I became saved. I had not lifted my hands to foreign Gods. The self-defense list could have continued had it not been for this scripture that He laid in my spirit:

The seed that fell among thorns stands for those who hear, but as they go on their way they are choked by life's worries, riches, and pleasures, and they do not mature. Luke 8:14 (NIV)

The Lord made me to take a proper look at my heart as though in the mirror. I had to see myself not as I thought I was but as He clearly sees. Truth is that we all have our ideals, what we are expecting from God as we wait on Him. It seems that as I grew older my perceived worth grew in my own eyes and I started building up an image of what kind of a man deserved me. You see, in my eyes and those of the people who loved me,

I was the "it" girl. I religiously believed that anybody who married me would be honoured and not the other way round. My first idol was myself and I thought more highly of myself than I should have. I am not down playing my worth, by no means. I am trying to show you that sometimes we build up so much around ourselves and forget that it is God who places worth on an individual.

It is not my virginity, my anointing, or all the works I had done in the name of the Lord that added to my worth. My worth was simply put on me by the act of love on Calvary. When He took the form of a servant it was so that I could have worth in Him. Some brothers and so many sisters have turned down prospects not because the Lord said to but because the man did not live up to the image/idol they created in their hearts. If you are royalty and a princess through Christ what makes you not see the prince in the other through Christ? The Lord told me that if He were to speak to me about who He had for me I would not be able to hear His voice because my ideals have become idols that would choke any word He spoke.

This brings me to the ideals we have built up inside our hearts in the form of "the list". I am not against having a list of the things you hope the Lord will give you in a man, not at all. It is a vision and the Lord encourages us to write the vision down plainly but every desire must be yielded to God. Simply put, our list is our desire or our will. We want a tall man, dark or light, one who fears the Lord, he must have a lot of money, must be compassionate, good looking, he must have at least a house and a car, and so the list goes on. Your desire or ideals become idols the moment you cling to them without surrendering them to God. "Do not settle for less" – we often preach this. What does that even mean, though? The actual fact is that settling for less is going for anything that is outside the will of God.

When God told me to remove the idols in my heart He was simply saying that I have not surrendered myself and my will to Him. I said I wanted a man who feared the Lord but in actual fact what I wanted was every other thing in the list. Was it surprising that I was approached by these guys in nice flashy cars with only a form of godliness and no fear of the Lord?

I had to do the most painful thing, I had to give up the picture of the man that I wanted. I had to give up the picture of the lofty princess in me and allow God to redefine my worth and what I ought to be looking for. It's a painful thing to surrender what you desire with all your heart but the end result is all worth it. Basically, God wants you to choose Him! Letting go of your claws on that thing you most desire and saying, "Lord I trust you with my heart and my life, give me what You know is best for me." That's a destruction of idols and an act of choosing God.

Jesus Christ at the Garden of Gethsemane was praying, knowing that what was before Him was extreme torture, humiliation, and death.. He cried out to the Father to take the cup away from Him, He desired to be spared of what was ahead. Then He uttered the words that bring perspective to me every time: "Yet, not My will but Yours be done." He was choosing God and His will above His pain and, ultimately, above Himself. To live a victorious and God-centered life we are to have this mindset of choosing God's will above our own, no matter how painful.

As you are waiting on the Lord I want to challenge you to dare look at yourself before the Lord. This is a step of maturity, to want what God wants and nothing less. I don't just mean lip service because you see a lot of people saying they are waiting on God but they are not. They are just passing time, hoping to catch the next big fish. If you are honest and want to wait right, allow God to take you through this process. Spend time with Him and ask Him to reveal you to yourself. This is not a one-day process, trust me.

Idols are a stubborn stronghold and so much undoing will be needed. Ask the Lord to uproot any idols that are in your heart, especially during this area of waiting on marriage. Write down every impression the Lord lays on your heart and then confess to God that this has been a sin before Him. If you are to write any list, let it be one that can be given back to God. Build again with God and I can assure you a building that will last.

The appointed time

I was now thirty-three years and I was still single. In the waiting season we can all testify that there are those moments where your confidence in the fulfillment of the promise is high and then there are also moments where the opposite takes over. This year for me was a hopeful year with God's promises refreshed in my spirit. There were those who were approaching me and I must say that more than ever I was afraid. I had moments of fear that I would miss the Lord's voice. What if I choose wrong? Decisions had to be made and most were easier to make than others. I had to make sure that I was not emotional about my decision and at the same time I had to make sure I did not depend on mere reasoning. I wanted to be led by God.

When I met my now husband we became friends and I felt we connected spiritually and intellectually. When I started considering him, I involved some friends and leaders who would pray along with me and offer good counsel. This brought so much wisdom. It was only after I had heard the Lord speaking to me that I accepted his proposal and we began our courtship.

It was time to show compassion on me and my Lord did that in a great way. I had met the man of my dreams, the one that the Lord had kept for me until it was time. Oh what a great fulfillment to receive from the Lord a long-awaited promise. Nothing compares to it! As the Lord often does, He went outside my confines only to give me what was best for me. The Lord knows us very well and when He blesses us He goes above and beyond our expectations.

One year and nine months later I married the man I had waited for. I will not sell a fairytale romance story but God's love story. I had been taught and am still learning that marriage is gold. Like gold, you will never find the treasure on the surface; one has to dig deep beneath to find it. God did not bring together perfect individuals but He joined two individuals who have the potential to love each other perfectly if they submit fully to God's ways. He married individuals whose strengths complement the other's weaknesses. He then poured on us so much grace for a marriage that will glorify Him.

I remember prior to meeting my now husband being so worried about having waited for so long. There were those days when I sat down with a piece of paper, counting my age, and estimating that I would be married at a certain age, seeing that the man had not come. I would then start thinking about children, whether or not I would be able to have any, and when God finally blesses me with children whether I would be a granny by the time they reach twenty years. I would literally have a panic attack at these thoughts. I have learned to observe God and to be thoughtful and I am so blown away by His ways.

I have seen Him have His way in my life, I have seen Him break through in the most powerful ways. Within one year I said "I do" to the most amazing man I know, I gave birth to a beautiful baby girl, and in the same year found out that I was pregnant again, expecting another child! I have seen the enemy trying to fight and abort each of these promises but I have known the Lord to raise the standard against the enemy. My time of waiting in these areas of life is over and the Lord has preserved every promise by His own mighty hand.

Two weeks before my wedding day I found out that my father had passed away. I was torn apart; I had wanted so much for him to witness the culmination of it all. He had seen my struggles and shared in my pains as a father. I could never have words enough to express the pain I experienced. We laid him to rest six days before my wedding day. The wedding was almost cancelled but I thank the Lord who ministered to my mother and my family to allow it to continue. All of us were torn, my mother especially, but that great woman laid aside her grief to let me have that day which we all knew was long waited for. If that is not love, I don't know what else is.

I want to encourage you to hold on because the one you are trusting in is faithful. I can boldly say that I am glad I waited on the Lord and I have no regrets. I am reaping the benefits of having waited. There is a tendency to compare oneself with others whom you feel have gone ahead of you. You may feel unfavoured compared to that one person whose life seems to flourish. That is a lie from the enemy, the Lord loves us all, He laid His life down as a demonstration of His love for all, not just one person but all who believed in Him. This includes you. He has plans to prosper you and is committed to fulfilling every word that He has spoken over you. Just be diligent in following after Him.

The Lord will redeem the times that you have lost. All the thoughts of feeling left behind and giving up hope on ever meeting up with those you are looking at are a cry to the Lord's ears. When He finally does it for you, you will be blown away! He will have restored all that has been stolen and cause you to catch up to those who you thought had gone ahead of you at the snap of a finger. He owns all things because He created them all. He, who is the author of time, can *never* be late, ever!

It is not on a man or woman we wait on but on God. We are waiting on Him to perform His word and the Bible tells us that none of His word is void, He watches over His word to see that it does what He sent it to do. Glory to God! He will do it for you.

The prayer

Father, in the name of Jesus Christ we have come before Your throne. We carry nothing of our own that will qualify us to stand with boldness before You, nothing but Christ Jesus. We thank You that You hear us when we pray and that even before our lips can utter any word You have already read it all in our hearts. We are grateful that You are God and not man, that You are true and dependable, everlasting Father.

Lord I pray for every woman/man that has read this story of my life, although to be honest it is not my story but an expression of Your handiwork in me. I thank You for all that You have taken your child through and I celebrate the struggles that she/he has had to endure because I know that it is the expression of how much You love them. You love them enough, Lord, to desire an eternity with them in your paradise. You have loved them enough to set them apart, making their journey peculiar. Thank You for calling them before they were born, thank You for setting them apart for a greater purpose of revealing Christ to them and through them. Lord I bless you, Lord I bless you.

Right now, Lord, I ask that You would reach out to them, to

their feeble knees I ask that you would breathe new strength. Cause them to stand once again even in the face of trials. To the one whose voice of confidence in who You say they are has diminished along the way, let Your authority come over them. Let there been a roaring like a lion coming out of their mouths. Let boldness arise because greater is He that is in them than he that is in the world. To the one whose vision and sense of identity has been thwarted by life's circumstances, find them Lord. Open hearts and spiritual eyes and cause them to dream dreams and see visions. Open ears that they may hear afresh from You, God. Revive them Lord, I pray.

Search for the broken and the discouraged and speak life once again in the name of Jesus. I speak life upon every dry bone. Into every life walking around without hope like the dead I declare the Spirit of God upon you. Lord breathe on your child Your mighty breath so they may come alive again.

For the one who has walked so far away that they cannot trace their steps back to You, Lord I pray right now that You would find them by Your mercy. Though their sins be red as scarlet, You promised that by Your blood they can be washed as white as snow. Speak the truth that they may know that there is no point beyond redemption as long as we have breath. Remind them, Lord, that we can never hide away from Your presence, even in our darkest hour, God, You are there. I call them back to You, Lord. In the name of Jesus, I speak strength unexplainable, I speak hope unfathomable, and I declare freedom from the chains of lies. Pour Your unrelenting love that knows no bounds. Showers of Your unmerited love I speak over them, Lord, Your redeeming love claims them as Your own and that they are. Lord, wipe away every tear, give assurance that even in times when they felt rejected and forsaken by You that You were there at every step and will continue to be. Remind them that they are Your beloved, that all that they are is inscribed at the palm of Your hands.

It is a dawn of new things, Lord, and a mighty army arises of those who will stand for You unashamed. Give each of us a testimony, an encounter that will forever change our lives. Lord we trust You, Lord we believe in You and Lord our hope is in You alone.

Thank you, glorious God, blessed be Your name. In Jesus' name we have prayed. Amen

Now go in the strength of the Lord. You are loved by God immeasurably.

You are Royal.

The End

About the author

Andiswa Jezile Oludare holds a Bachelor of Pharmacy degree from the University of KwaZulu-Natal. She is a speaker and the founder for Colour Me Royal(CMR), an organisation that organises conferences as a platform for preaching the Gospel and steering hearts towards a radical followership of Jesus Christ.

www.ingramcontent.com/pod-product-compliance
Lightning Source LLC
Chambersburg PA
CBHW021934040426
42448CB00008B/1058